EVERYMAN'S LIBRARY
POCKET POETS

EVERYMAN,
I WILL GO WITH THEE
AND BE THY GUIDE,
IN THY MOST NEED
TO GO BY THY SIDE

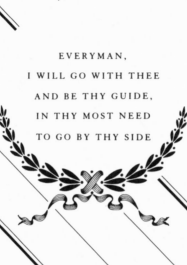

MARVELL

·················

POEMS

EVERYMAN'S LIBRARY
POCKET POETS

Alfred A. Knopf New York London Toronto

THIS IS A BORZOI BOOK
PUBLISHED BY ALFRED A. KNOPF

This selection by Peter Washington first published in
Everyman's Library, 2004
Copyright © 2004 by Everyman's Library

US website: www.randomhouse.com/everymans

ISBN 1-4000-4252-6 (US)
1-84159-761-9 (UK)

A CIP catalogue record for this book is available from the British Library

Typography by Peter B. Willberg
Typeset in the UK by AccComputing, North Barrow, Somerset
Printed and bound in Germany by GGP Media, Pössneck

CONTENTS

NOTE ON THE TEXT

This edition of Marvell's poems retains the author's spelling and his use of capitals and italics. In a few cases, commas have been added for the sake of clarity. It should be remembered that seventeenth-century punctuation and orthography were inconsistent.

Four translations from Marvell's Latin verse have been included for the sake of the light they throw on his English poems. *Dew* and the second version of *The Garden* (page 59) appear in versions by William A. McQueen and Kiffin A. Rockwell, courtesy the University of North Carolina Press. The 'Epigram on the two Mountains of *Amos-Cliff* and *Bilborough*' and 'Upon an Eunuch; a Poet' are translated by A. B. Grosart.

Some scholars dispute Marvell's authorship of 'The Second Advice', 'Clarindon's House-warming' and 'The Vows.'

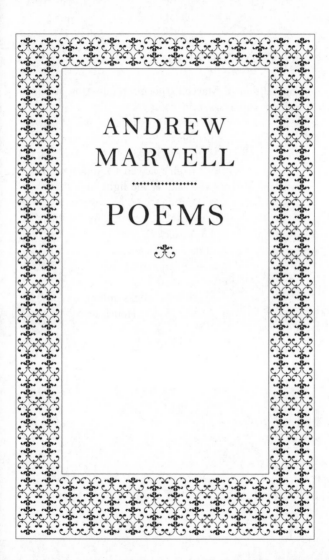

ANDREW MARVELL

································

POEMS

OF LOVE

THE DEFINITION OF LOVE

My Love is of a birth as rare
As 'tis for object strange and high:
It was begotten by despair
Upon Impossibility.

Magnanimous Despair alone
Could show me so divine a thing,
Where feeble Hope could ne'r have flown
But vainly flapt its Tinsel Wing.

And yet I quickly might arrive
Where my extended Soul is fixt,
But Fate does Iron wedges drive,
And alwaies crouds it self betwixt.

For Fate with jealous Eye does see
Two perfect Loves; nor lets them close;
Their union would her ruine be,
And her Tyrannick pow'r depose.

And therefore her Decrees of Steel
Us as the distant Poles have plac'd,
(Though Loves whole World on us doth wheel)
Not by themselves to be embrac'd.

Unless the giddy Heaven fall,
And Earth some new Convulsion tear;
And, us to joyn, the World should all
Be cramp'd into a *Planisphere*.

As Lines so Loves *oblique* may well
Themselves in every Angle greet:
But ours so truly *Paralel*,
Though infinite can never meet.

Therefore the Love which us doth bind,
But Fate so enviously debarrs,
Is the Conjunction of the Mind,
And Opposition of the Stars.

THE MATCH

Nature had long a Treasure made
    Of all her choisest store;
Fearing, when She should be decay'd,
    To beg in vain for more.

Her *Orientest* Colours there,
    And Essences most pure,
With sweetest Perfumes hoarded were,
    All as she thought secure.

She seldom them unlock'd, or us'd,
    But with the nicest care;
For, with one grain of them diffus'd,
    She could the World repair.

But likeness soon together drew
    What she did sep'rate lay;
Of which one perfect Beauty grew,
    And that was *Celia*.

Love wisely had of long fore-seen
    That he must once grow old;
And therefore stor'd a Magazine,
    To save him from the cold.

He kept the several Cells repleat
   With Nitre thrice refin'd;
The Naphta's and the Sulphur's heat,
   And all that burns the Mind.

He fortifi'd the double Gate,
   And rarely thither came;
For, with one Spark of these, he streight
   All Nature could inflame.

Till, by vicinity so long,
   A nearer Way they sought;
And, grown magnetically strong,
   Into each other wrought.

Thus all his fewel did unite
   To make one fire high:
None ever burn'd so hot, so bright:
   And *Celia* that am I.

So we alone the happy rest,
   Whilst all the World is poor,
And have within our Selves possest
   All Love's and Nature's store.

TO HIS COY MISTRESS

    Had we but World enough, and Time,
This coyness Lady were no crime.
We would sit down, and think which way
To walk, and pass our long Loves Day.
Thou by the *Indian Ganges* side
Should'st Rubies find: I by the Tide
Of *Humber* would complain. I would
Love you ten years before the Flood:
And you should, if you please, refuse
Till the Conversion of the *Jews*.
My vegetable Love should grow
Vaster than Empires, and more slow.
An hundred years should go to praise
Thine Eyes, and on thy Forehead Gaze.
Two hundred to adore each Breast:
But thirty thousand to the rest.
An Age at least to every part,
And the last Age should show your Heart.
For Lady you deserve this State;
Nor would I love at lower rate.
    But at my back I alwaies hear
Times winged Charriot hurrying near:
And yonder all before us lye
Deserts of vast Eternity.
Thy Beauty shall no more be found;

Nor, in thy marble Vault, shall sound
My ecchoing Song; then Worms shall try
That long preserv'd Virginity:
And your quaint Honour turn to dust;
And into ashes all my Lust.
The Grave's a fine and private place,
But none I think do there embrace.
   Now therefore, while the youthful hew
Sits on thy skin like morning dew,
And while thy willing Soul transpires
At every pore with instant Fires,
Now let us sport us while we may;
And now, like am'rous birds of prey,
Rather at once our Time devour,
Than languish in his slow-chapt pow'r.
Let us roll all our Strength, and all
Our sweetness, up into one Ball:
And tear our Pleasures with rough strife,
Thorough the Iron gates of Life.
Thus, though we cannot make our Sun
Stand still, yet we will make him run.

THE FAIR SINGER

To make a final conquest of all me,
Love did compose so sweet an Enemy,
In whom both Beauties to my death agree,
Joyning themselves in fatal Harmony;
That while she with her Eyes my Heart does bind,
She with her Voice might captivate my Mind.

I could have fled from One but singly fair:
My dis-intangled Soul it self might save,
Breaking the curled trammels of her hair.
But how should I avoid to be her Slave,
Whose subtile Art invisibly can wreath
My Fetters of the very Air I breathe?

It had been easie fighting in some plain,
Where Victory might hang in equal choice.
But all resistance against her is vain,
Who has th' advantage both of Eyes and Voice.
And all my Forces needs must be undone,
She having gained both the Wind and Sun.

EYES AND TEARS

How wisely Nature did decree,
With the same Eyes to weep and see!
That, having view'd the object vain,
They might be ready to complain.

And, since the Self-deluding Sight
In a false Angle takes each hight;
These Tears which better measure all,
Like wat'ry Lines and Plummets fall.

Two Tears, which Sorrow long did weigh
Within the Scales of either Eye,
And then paid out in equal Poise,
Are the true price of all my Joyes.

What in the World most fair appears,
Yea even Laughter, turns to Tears:
And all the Jewels which we prize,
Melt in these Pendants of the Eyes.

I have through every Garden been,
Amongst the Red, the White, the Green;
And yet, from all the flow'rs I saw,
No Hony, but these Tears could draw.

So the all-seeing Sun each day
Distills the World with Chymick Ray;
But finds the Essence only Show'rs,
Which straight in pity back he poures.

Yet happy they whom Grief doth bless,
That weep the more, and see the less:
And, to preserve their Sight more true,
Bath still their Eyes in their own Dew.

So *Magdalen*, in Tears more wise
Dissolv'd those captivating Eyes,
Whose liquid Chaines could flowing meet
To fetter her Redeemers feet.

Not full sailes hasting loaden home,
Nor the chast Ladies pregnant Womb,
Nor *Cynthia* Teeming show's so fair,
As two Eyes swoln with weeping are.

The sparkling Glance that shoots Desire,
Drench'd in these Waves, does lose its fire.
Yea oft the Thund'rer pitty takes
And here the hissing Lightning slakes.

The Incense was to Heaven dear,
Not as a Perfume, but a Tear.
And Stars shew lovely in the Night,
But as they seem the Tears of Light.

Ope then mine Eyes your double Sluice,
And practise so your noblest Use.
For others too can see, or sleep;
But only humane Eyes can weep.

Now like two Clouds dissolving, drop,
And at each Tear in Distance stop:
Now like two Fountains trickle down:
Now like two floods o'return and drown.

Thus let your Streams o'reflow your Springs,
Till Eyes and Tears be the same things:
And each the other's difference bears;
These weeping Eyes, those seeing Tears.

THE UNFORTUNATE LOVER

Alas, how pleasant are their dayes
With whom the Infant Love yet playes!
Sorted by pairs, they still are seen
By Fountains cool, and Shadows green.
But soon these Flames do lose their light,
Like Meteors of a Summers night:
Nor can they to that Region climb,
To make impression upon Time.

'Twas in a Shipwrack, when the Seas
Rul'd, and the Winds did what they please,
That my poor Lover floting lay,
And, e're brought forth, was cast away:
Till at the last the master-Wave
Upon the Rock his Mother drave;
And there she split against the Stone,
In a *Cesarian Section*.

The Sea him lent these bitter Tears
Which at his Eyes he alwaies bears:
And from the Winds the Sighs he bore,
Which through his surging Breast do roar.
No Day he saw but that which breaks,
Through frighted Clouds in forked streaks.
While round the ratling Thunder hurl'd,
As at the Fun'ral of the World.

While Nature to his Birth presents
This masque of quarrelling Elements;
A num'rous fleet of Corm'rants black,
That sail'd insulting o're the Wrack,
Receiv'd into their cruel Care,
Th' unfortunate and abject Heir:
Guardians most fit to entertain
The Orphan of the *Hurricane.*

They fed him up with Hopes and Air,
Which soon digested to Despair.
And as one Corm'rant fed him, still
Another on his Heart did bill.
Thus while they famish him, and feast,
He both consumed, and increast:
And languished with doubtful Breath,
Th' *Amphibium* of Life and Death.

And now, when angry Heaven wou'd
Behold a spectacle of Blood,
Fortune and He are call'd to play
At sharp before it all the day:
And Tyrant Love his brest does ply
With all his wing'd Artillery.
Whilst he, betwixt the Flames and Waves,
Like *Ajax* the mad Tempest braves.

See how he nak'd and fierce does stand,
Cuffing the Thunder with one hand;
While with the other he does lock,
And grapple, with the stubborn Rock:
From which he with each Wave rebounds,
Torn into Flames, and ragg'd with Wounds.
And all he saies, a Lover drest
In his own Blood does relish best.

This is the only *Banneret*
That ever Love created yet:
Who though, by the Malignant Starrs,
Forced to live in Storms and Warrs;
Yet dying leaves a Perfume here,
And Musick within every Ear:
And he in Story only rules,
In a Field *Sable* a Lover *Gules*.

THE GALLERY

Clora come view my Soul, and tell
Whether I have contriv'd it well.
Now all its several lodgings lye
Compos'd into one Gallery;
And the great *Arras*-hangings, made
Of various Faces, by are laid;
That, for all furniture, you'l find
Only your Picture in my Mind.

Here Thou art painted in the Dress
Of an Inhumane Murtheress;
Examining upon our Hearts
Thy fertile Shop of cruel Arts:
Engines more keen than ever yet
Adorned Tyrants Cabinet;
Of which the most tormenting are
Black Eyes, red Lips, and curled Hair.

But, on the other side, th'art drawn
Like to *Aurora* in the Dawn;
When in the East she slumb'ring lyes,
And stretches out her milky Thighs;
While all the morning Quire does sing,
And *Manna* falls, and Roses spring;
And, at thy Feet, the wooing Doves
Sit perfecting their harmless Loves.

Like an Enchantress here thou show'st,
Vexing thy restless Lover's Ghost;
And, by a Light obscure, dost rave
Over his Entrails, in the Cave;
Divining thence, with horrid Care,
How long thou shalt continue fair;
And (when inform'd) them throw'st away,
To be the greedy Vultur's prey.

But, against that, thou sit'st a float
Like *Venus* in her pearly Boat.
The *Halcyons*, calming all that's nigh,
Betwixt the Air and Water fly.
Or, if some rowling Wave appears,
A Mass of Ambergris it bears.
Nor blows more Wind than what may well
Convoy the Perfume to the Smell.

These Pictures and a thousand more,
Of Thee, my Gallery do store;
In all the Forms thou can'st invent
Either to please me, or torment:
For thou alone to people me,
Art grown a num'rous Colony;
And a Collection choicer far
Than or *White-hall's*, or *Mantua's* were.

But, of these Pictures and the rest,
That at the Entrance likes me best:
Where the same Posture, and the Look
Remains, with which I first was took.
A tender Shepherdess, whose Hair
Hangs loosely playing in the Air,
Transplanting Flow'rs from the green Hill,
To crown her Head, and Bosome fill.

AMETAS AND *THESTYLIS*
MAKING HAY-ROPES

Ametas
Think'st Thou that this Love can stand,
Whilst Thou still dost say me nay?
Love unpaid does soon disband:
Love binds Love as Hay binds Hay.

Thestylis
Think'st Thou that this Rope would twine
If we both should turn one way?
Where both parties so combine,
Neither Love will twist nor Hay.

Ametas
Thus you vain Excuses find,
Which your selves and us delay:
And Love tyes a Womans Mind
Looser than with Ropes of Hay.

Thestylis
What you cannot constant hope
Must be taken as you may.

Ametas
Then let's both lay by our Rope,
And go kiss within the Hay.

DAPHNIS AND CHLOE

Daphnis must from *Chloe* part:
Now is come the dismal Hour
That must all his Hopes devour,
All his Labour, all his Art.

Nature, her own Sexes foe,
Long had taught her to be coy:
But she neither knew t'enjoy,
Nor yet let her Lover go.

But, with this sad News supriz'd,
Soon she let that Niceness fall;
And would gladly yield to all,
So it had his stay compriz'd.

Nature so her self does use
To lay by her wonted State,
Lest the World should separate;
Sudden Parting closer glews.

He, well read in all the wayes
By which men their Siege maintain,
Knew not that the Fort to gain
Better 'twas the Siege to raise.

But he came so full possest
With the Grief of Parting thence,
That he had not so much Sence
As to see he might be blest.

Till Love in her Language breath'd
Words she never spake before;
But than Legacies no more
To a dying Man bequeath'd.

For, Alas, the time was spent,
Now the latest minut's run
When poor *Daphnis* is undone,
Between Joy and Sorrow rent.

At that *Why*, that *Stay my Dear*,
His disorder'd Locks he tare;
And with rouling Eyes did glare,
And his cruel Fate forswear.

As the Soul of one scarce dead,
With the shrieks of Friends aghast,
Looks distracted back in hast,
And then streight again is fled.

So did wretched *Daphnis* look,
Frighting her he loved most.
At the last, this Lovers Ghost
Thus his Leave resolved took.

Are my Hell and Heaven Joyn'd
More to torture him that dies?
Could departure not suffice,
But that you must then grow kind?

Ah my *Chloe* how have I
Such a wretched minute found,
When thy Favours should me wound
More than all thy Cruelty?

So to the condemned Wight
The delicious Cup we fill;
And allow him all he will,
For his last and short Delight.

But I will not now begin
Such a Debt unto my Foe;
Nor to my Departure owe
What my Presence could not win.

Absence is too much alone:
Better 'tis to go in peace,
Than my Losses to increase
By a late Fruition.

Why should I enrich my Fate?
'Tis a Vanity to wear,
For my Executioner,
Jewels of so high a rate.

Rather I away will pine
In a manly stubborness
Than be fatted up express
For the *Canibal* to dine.

Whilst this grief does thee disarm,
All th' Enjoyment of our Love
But the ravishment would prove
Of a Body dead while warm.

And I parting should appear
Like the Gourmand *Hebrew* dead,
While with Quailes and *Manna* fed,
He does through the Desert err;

Or the Witch that midnight wakes
For the Fern, whose magick Weed
In one minute casts the Seed,
And invisible him makes.

Gentler times for Love are ment:
Who for parting pleasure strain
Gather Roses in the rain,
Wet themselves and spoil their Scent.

Farewel therefore all the fruit
Which I could from Love receive:
Joy will not with Sorrow weave,
Nor will I this Grief pollute.

Fate I come, as dark, as sad,
As thy Malice could desire;
Yet bring with me all the Fire
That Love in his Torches had.

At these words away he broke;
As who long has praying ly'n,
To his Heads-man makes the Sign,
And receives the parting stroke.

But hence Virgins all beware.
Last night he with *Phlogis* slept;
This night for *Dorinda* kept;
And but rid to take the Air.

Yet he does himself excuse,
Nor indeed without a Cause.
For, according to the Lawes,
Why did *Chloe* once refuse?

CLORINDA AND DAMON

C. *Damon* come drive thy flocks this way.
D. No: 'tis too late they went astray.
C. I have a grassy Scutcheon spy'd,
Where *Flora* blazons all her pride.
The Grass I aim to feast thy Sheep:
The Flow'rs I for thy Temples keep.
D. Grass withers; and the Flow'rs too fade.
C. Seize the short Joyes then, ere they vade.
Seest thou that unfrequented Cave?
D. That den? C. Loves Shrine. D. But
Virtue's Grave.
C. In whose cool bosome we may lye
Safe from the sun. D. Not Heaven's Eye.
C. Near this, a Fountaines liquid Bell
Tinkles within the concave Shell.
D. Might a Soul bath there and be clean,
Or slake its Drought? C. What is't you mean?
D. These once had been enticing things,
Clorinda, Pastures, Caves, and Springs.
C. And what late change? D. The other day
Pan met me. C. What did great *Pan* say?
D. Words that transcend poor Shepherds skill;
But He e'er since my Songs does fill:
And his Name swells my slender Oate.
C. Sweet must *Pan* sound in *Damons* Note.

D.   *Clorinda's* voice might make it sweet.
C.   Who would not in *Pan's* Praises meet?

Chorus
Of Pan *the flowry Pastures sing,*
Caves eccho, and the Fountains ring.
Sing then while he doth us inspire;
For all the World is our Pan's *Quire.*

YOUNG LOVE

Come little Infant, Love me now,
    While thine unsuspected years
Clear thine aged Fathers brow
    From cold Jealousie and Fears.

Pretty surely 'twere to see
    By young Love old Time beguil'd:
While our Sportings are as free
    As the Nurses and the Child.

Common Beauties stay fifteen;
    Such as yours should swifter move;
Whose fair Blossoms are too green
    Yet for Lust, but not for Love.

Love as much the snowy Lamb
    Or the wanton kid does prize,
As the lusty Bull or Ram,
    For his morning Sacrifice.

Now then love me: time may take
    Thee before thy time away:
Of this Need wee'l Virtue make,
    And learn Love before we may.

So we win of doubtful Fate;
    And, if good she to us meant,
We that Good shall antedate,
    Or, if ill, that Ill prevent.

Thus as Kingdomes, frustrating
    Other Titles to their Crown,
In the craddle crown their King,
    So all Forraign Claims to drown,

So, to make all Rivals vain,
    Now I crown thee with my Love:
Crown me with thy Love again,
    And we both shall Monarchs prove.

OF GARDENS

THE GARDEN

How vainly men themselves amaze
To win the Palm, the Oke, or Bayes;
And their uncessant Labours see
Crown'd from some single Herb or Tree,
Whose short and narrow verged Shade
Does prudently their Toyles upbraid;
While all Flow'rs and all Trees do close
To weave the Garlands of repose.

Fair quiet, have I found thee here,
And Innocence thy Sister dear!
Mistaken long, I sought you then
In busie Companies of Men.
Your sacred Plants, if here below,
Only among the Plants will grow.
Society is all but rude,
To this delicious Solitude.

No white nor red was ever seen
So am'rous as this lovely green.
Fond Lovers, cruel as their Flame,
Cut in these Trees their Mistress name.
Little, Alas, they know, or heed,
How far these Beauties Hers exceed!
Fair Trees! where s'ere your barkes I wound,
No Name shall but your own be found.

When we have run our Passions heat,
Love hither makes his best retreat.
The *Gods*, that mortal Beauty chase,
Still in a Tree did end their race.
Apollo hunted *Daphne* so,
Only that She might Laurel grow.
And *Pan* did after *Syrinx* speed,
Not as a Nymph, but for a Reed.

What wond'rous Life in this I lead!
Ripe Apples drop about my head;
The Luscious Clusters of the Vine
Upon my Mouth do crush their Wine;
The Nectaren, and curious Peach,
Into my hands themselves do reach;
Stumbling on Melons, as I pass,
Insnar'd with Flow'rs, I fall on Grass.

Mean while the Mind, from pleasures less,
Withdraws into its happiness:
The Mind, that Ocean where each kind
Does streight its own resemblance find;
Yet it creates, transcending these,
Far other Worlds, and other Seas;
Annihilating all that's made
To a green Thought in a green Shade.

Here at the Fountains sliding foot,
Or at some Fruit-tree's mossy root,
Casting the Bodies Vest aside,
My Soul into the boughs does glide:
There like a Bird it sits, and sings,
Then whets, and combs its silver Wings;
And, till prepar'd for longer flight,
Waves in its Plumes the various Light.

Such was that happy Garden-state,
While Man there walk'd without a Mate:
After a Place so pure, and sweet,
What other Help could yet be meet!
But 'twas beyond a Mortal's share
To wander solitary there:
Two Paradises 'twere in one
To live in Paradise alone.

How well the skilful Gardner drew
Of flow'rs and herbes this Dial new;
Where from above the milder Sun
Does through a fragrant Zodiack run;
And, as it works, th' industrious Bee
Computes its time as well as we.
How could such sweet and wholsome Hours
Be reckon'd but with herbs and flow'rs!

THE MOWER AGAINST GARDENS

Luxurious Man, to bring his Vice in use,
    Did after him the World seduce:
And from the fields the Flow'rs and Plants allure,
    Where Nature was most plain and pure.
He first enclos'd within the Gardens square
    A dead and standing pool of Air:
And a more luscious Earth for them did knead,
    Which stupifi'd them while it fed.
The Pink grew then as double as his Mind;
    The nutriment did change the kind.
With strange perfumes he did the Roses taint,
    And Flow'rs themselves were taught to paint.
The Tulip, white, did for complexion seek;
    And learn'd to interline its cheek:
Its Onion root they then so high did hold,
    That one was for a Meadow sold.
Another World was search'd, through Oceans new,
    To find the *Marvel of Peru.*
And yet these Rarities might be allow'd,
    To Man, that sov'raign thing and proud;
Had he not dealt between the Bark and Tree,
    Forbidden mixtures there to see.
No Plant now knew the Stock from which it came;
    He grafts upon the Wild the Tame:
That the uncertain and adult'rate fruit

Might put the Palate in dispute.
His green *Seraglio* has its Eunuchs too;
  Lest any Tyrant him out-doe.
And in the Cherry he does Nature vex,
  To procreate without a Sex.
'Tis all enforc'd; the Fountain and the Grot;
  While the sweet Fields do lye forgot:
Where willing Nature does to all dispence
  A wild and fragrant Innocence:
And *Fauns* and *Faryes* do the Meadows till,
  More by their presence than their skill.
Their Statues polish'd by some ancient hand,
  May to adorn the Gardens stand:
But howso'ere the Figures do excel,
  The *Gods* themselves with us do dwell.

DAMON THE MOWER

Heark how the Mower *Damon* Sung.
With love of *Juliana* stung!
While ev'ry thing did seem to paint
The Scene more fit for his complaint.
Like her fair Eyes the day was fair;
But scorching like his am'rous Care.
Sharp like his Sythe his Sorrow was,
And wither'd like his Hopes the Grass.

Oh what unusual Hearts are here,
Which thus our Sun-burn'd Meadows fear!
The Grass-hopper its pipe gives ore;
And hamstring'd Frogs can dance no more.
But in the brook the green Frog wades;
And Grass-hoppers seek out the shades.
Only the Snake, that kept within,
Now glitters in its second skin.

This heat the Sun could never raise,
Nor Dog-star so inflame's the dayes.
It from an higher Beauty grow'th,
Which burns the Fields and Mower both:
Which mads the Dog, and makes the Sun
Hotter than his own *Phaeton*.
Not *July* causeth these Extremes,
But *Juliana's* scorching beams.

Tell me where I may pass the Fires
Of the hot day, or hot desires.
To what cool Cave shall I descend,
Or to what gelid Fountain bend?
Alas! I look for Ease in vain,
When Remedies themselves complain.
No moisture but my Tears do rest,
Nor Cold but in her Icy Breast.

How long wilt Thou, fair Shepheardess,
Esteem me, and my Presents less?
To Thee the harmless Snake I bring,
Disarmed of its teeth and sting.
To Thee *Chameleons* changing-hue,
And Oak leaves tipt with hony-dew.
Yet Thou ungrateful hast not sought
Nor what they are, nor who them brought.

I am the Mower *Damon*, known
Through all the Medows I have mown.
On me the Morn her dew distills
Before her darling Daffadils.
And, if at Noon my toil me heat,
The Sun himself licks off my Sweat.
While, going home, the Ev'ning sweet
In cowslip-water bathes my feet.

49

What, though the piping Shepherd stock
The plains with an unnumber'd Flock,
This Sithe of mine discovers wide
More ground than all his Sheep do hide.
With this the golden fleece I shear
Of all these Closes ev'ry Year.
And though in Wooll more poor than they,
Yet am I richer far in Hay.

Nor am I so deform'd to sight,
If in my Sithe I looked right;
In which I see my Picture done,
As in a crescent Moon the Sun.
The deathless Fairyes take me oft
To lead them in their Danses soft:
And, when I tune my self to sing,
About me they contract their Ring.

How happy might I still have mow'd,
Had not Love here his Thistles sow'd!
But now I all the day complain,
Joyning my Labour to my Pain;
And with my Sythe cut down the Grass,
Yet still my Grief is where it was:
But, when the Iron blunter grows,
Sighing I whet my Sythe and Woes.

While thus he threw his Elbow round,
Depopulating all the Ground,
And, with his whistling Sythe, does cut
Each stroke between the Earth and Root,
The edged Stele by careless chance
Did into his own Ankle glance:
And there among the Grass fell down,
By his own Sythe, the Mower mown.

Alas! said He, these hurts are slight
To those that dye by Loves despight.
With Shepherds-purse, and Clowns-all-heal,
The Blood I stanch, and Wound I seal.
Only for him no Cure is found,
Whom *Julianas* Eyes do wound.
'Tis death alone that this must do:
For Death thou art a Mower too.

THE MOWER'S SONG

My Mind was once the true survey
Of all these Medows fresh and gay;
And in the greeness of the Grass
Did see its Hopes as in a Glass;
When *Juliana* came, and She
What I do to the Grass, does to my Thoughts and Me.

But these, while I with Sorrow pine,
Grew more luxuriant still and fine;
That not one Blade of Grass you spy'd,
But had a Flower on either side;
When *Juliana* came, and She
What I do to the Grass, does to my Thoughts and Me.

Unthankful Medows, could you so
A fellowship so true forego.
And in your gawdy May-games meet,
While I lay trodden under feet?
When *Juliana* came, and She
What I do to the Grass, does to my Thoughts and Me.

But what you in Compassion ought
Shall now by my Revenge be wrought:
And Flow'rs, and Grass, and I and all,
Will in one common Ruine fall.

    For *Juliana* comes, and She
What I do to the Grass, does to my Thoughts and Me.

    And thus, ye Meadows, which have been
    Companions of my thoughts more green,
    Shall now the Heraldry become
    With which I shall adorn my Tomb;
    For *Juliana* comes, and She
What I do to the Grass, does to my Thoughts and Me.

THE MOWER TO THE GLO-WORMS

Ye living Lamps, by whose dear light
The Nightingale does sit so late,
And studying all the Summer-night,
Her matchless Songs does meditate;

Ye Country Comets, that portend
No War, nor Princes funeral,
Shining unto no higher end
Than to presage the Grasses fall;

Ye Glo-worms, whose officious Flame
To wandring Mowers shows the way.
That in the Night have lost their aim,
And after foolish Fires do stray;

Your courteous Lights in vain you waste,
Since *Juliana* here is come,
For She my Mind hath so displac'd
That I shall never find my home.

THE PICTURE OF LITTLE *T. C.* IN
A PROSPECT OF FLOWERS

See with what simplicity
This Nimph begins her golden daies!
In the green Grass she loves to lie,
And there with her fair Aspect tames
The Wilder flow'rs, and gives them names:
But only with the Roses playes;
             And them does tell
What Colour best becomes them, and what Smell.

Who can foretel for what high cause
This Darling of the Gods was born!
Yet this is She whose chaster Laws
The wanton Love shall one day fear,
And, under her command severe,
See his Bow broke and Ensigns torn.
             Happy, who can
Appease this virtuous Enemy of Man!

O then let me in time compound,
And parly with those conquering Eyes;
Ere they have try'd their force to wound,
Ere, with their glancing wheels, they drive
In Triumph over Hearts that strive,
And them that yield but more despise.

Let me be laid,
Where I may see thy Glories from some Shade.

Mean time, whilst every verdant thing
It self does at thy Beauty charm,
Reform the errours of the Spring;
Make that the Tulips may have share
Of sweetness, seeing they are fair;
And Roses of their thorns disarm:
                    But most procure
That Violets may a longer Age endure.

But O young beauty of the Woods,
Whom Nature courts with fruits and flow'rs,
Gather the Flow'rs, but spare the Buds;
Lest *Flora* angry at thy crime,
To kill her Infants in their prime,
Do quickly make th' Example Yours;
                    And, ere we see,
Nip in the blossome all our hopes and Thee.

BERMUDAS

Where the remote *Bermudas* ride
In th' Oceans bosome unespy'd,
From a small Boat, that row'd along,
The listning Winds receiv'd this Song.
    What should we do but sing his Praise
That led us through the watry Maze,
Unto an Isle so long unknown,
And yet far kinder than our own?
Where he the huge Sea-Monsters wracks
That lift the Deep upon their Backs.
He lands us on a grassy Stage;
Safe from the Storms, and Prelat's rage.
He gave us this eternal Spring,
Which here enamells every thing;
And sends the Fowl's to us in care,
On daily Visits through the Air.
He hangs in shades the Orange bright,
Like golden Lamps in a green Night.
And does in the Pomgranates close
Jewels more rich than *Ormus* shows.
He makes the Figs our mouths to meet;
And throws the Melons at our feet.
But Apples plants of such a price,
No Tree could ever bear them twice.
With Cedars, chosen by his hand,

From *Lebanon*, he stores the Land.
And makes the hollow Seas, that roar,
Proclaime the Ambergris on shoar.
He cast (of which we rather boast)
The Gospels Pearl upon our Coast.
And in these Rocks for us did frame
A Temple, where to sound his Name.
Oh let our Voice his Praise exalt,
Till it arrive at Heavens Vault:
Which thence (perhaps) rebounding, may
Eccho beyond the *Mexique Bay.*
Thus sung they, in the *English* boat,
An holy and a chearful Note,
And all the way, to guide their Chime,
With falling Oars they kept the time.

THE GARDEN (from the Latin)

What madness so stirs the heart of man?
Alas, madness for the Palm and the Laurel, or for the
      simple grass!
So that one tree will scarcely crown his curbless
      efforts,
Nor wholly circle his temples with its scanty leaves.
While at the same time, entwined in garlands of
      tranquil Quiet,
All flowers meet, and the virgin woods.

Fair Quiet, I hold you! And you, sister of Quiet,
Innocence! You a long time in temples, in cities
I sought in vain, and in the palaces of kings.
But you in the shaded silences of gardens, far off,
The green plants and like-colored shadow hide.

Oh, if I am ever allowed to profane your retreats,
Wandering about, faint, and panting for a better life,
Preserve your new citizen, and me, having attained my
      wish,
Leafy citizens, accept in the flowery kingdom.

Me also, you *Muses* – and I call you, omniscient
      Apollo, as witness –
Herds of men do not please, nor the roaring of the
      Circus,
Nor the bellowing of the Forum; but me the
      sanctuaries of spring,

59

And silent veneration draw, and solitary communion.
Whom does the grace of maidenly beauty not arrest?
Which, although it excels snows in whiteness and
    purple in redness,
Yet your green force (in my opinion) surpasses.
Hair cannot compete with leaves, nor arms with
    branches,
Nor are tremulous voices able to equal your
    whisperings.
  Ah, how often have I seen (Who would believe it?)
    cruel lovers
Carving the name of their mistress on bark, which is
    more worthy of love.
Nor was there a sense of shame for inscribing wounds
    on sacred trunks.
But I, if ever I shall have profaned your stocks,
No *Neaera, Chloe, Faustina, Corynna* shall be read:
But the name of each tree shall be written on its own
    bark.
O dear *plane tree, cypress, poplar, elm*!
  Here Love, his wings cast aside, walks about in
    sandals,
Laying aside his nerveless bows and hissing arrows,
And inverts his torches, nor does he wish to be feared;
Or he lies stretched out and sleeps on his quiver;
Nor will he hear, although Cytherea call;
Nor do idle dreams report previous iniquities.

60

The Gods rejoice, the Tyrant ceasing to rage,
And although they have known *nymphs* and *goddesses*
    many times,
Each one achieves his desires better now in a *tree*.
Jupiter, forgetful of his wife, languishes for the aged oak;
Juno has not suffered thus for another rival.
No traces dishonor the bed of *Vulcan*,
Nor is *Mars* mindful of *Venus* if the *ash* be present.
Apollo pursued beautiful *Daphne*
That she might become a *laurel*; but he had sought
    nothing more.
And though goat-footed *Pan* fell upon fleeing *Syrinx*,
This was that he might procure a sounding reed.
Desunt multa
And you, maker of the garden, shall not depart
    without a grateful song:
You who in the brief plants and joyous flowers have
    indicated
The growing hours and intervals of the day.
There the sun more bright passes through the
    fragrant signs;
And fleeing the fierce *Bull*, the *Crab's* threatening claw,
Glides toward the safe shadows of roses and violets.
And the sedulous bee, intent on its sweet labor,
Seems to mark its duties with the thyme as horologe.
O sweet lapse of time! O healthful ease!
    O hours worthy to be numbered in herbs and flowers!

61

OF BODY AND SOUL

ON A DROP OF DEW

See how the Orient Dew,
   Shed from the Bosom of the Morn
   Into the blowing Roses,
Yet careless of its Mansion new
For the clear Region where 'twas born,
   Round in its self incloses:
   And in its little Globes Extent
Frames as it can its native Element.
   How it the purple flow'r does slight,
      Scarce touching where it lyes,
   But gazing back upon the Skies,
      Shines with a mournful Light;
        Like its own Tear,
Because so long divided from the Sphear.
   Restless it roules and unsecure,
      Trembling lest it grow impure:
   Till the warm Sun pitty it's Pain,
And to the Skies exhale it back again.
      So the Soul, that Drop, that Ray
Of the clear Fountain of Eternal Day,
Could it within the humane flow'r be seen,
      Remembering still its former height,
      Shuns the sweet leaves and blossoms green;
      And, recollecting its own Light,
Does, in its pure and circling thoughts, express

The greater Heaven in an Heaven less.
    In how coy a Figure wound,
    Every way it turns away:
    So the World excluding round,
    Yet receiving in the Day.
    Dark beneath, but bright above:
    Here disdaining, there in Love.
  How loose and easie hence to go:
  How girt and ready to ascend.
  Moving but on a point below,
    It all about does upwards bend.
Such did the Manna's sacred Dew destil;
White, and intire, though congeal'd and chill.
Congeal'd on Earth: but does, dissolving, run
Into the Glories of th' Almighty Sun.

DEW (from the Latin)

See how a little jewel of Orient dew descends
And, sprung from the rosy breast to Dawn, flows onto
     the roses,
The flowers stand, opened in solicitous desire,
And strive to entice with their leaves.
Yet that drop, surveying the heights of its native
     sphere,
Disdains the painted threshold of its new dwelling.
And enclosed within its shining globe,
It shapes the waters of the ethereal sphere as it can.
See how it, more noble, scorns the odorous purple,
And scarely presses the soft resting place with its pure
     foot.
It looks up at the distant heavens with a long gaze,
And, desiring that place, hangs with a faint glow,
Sad, changed by sorrow into liquid sorrow,
It is spent, like a tear upon a rosy cheek.
Restless, how it trembles and quivers on its troubled
     couch,
And, as often as the air stirs with a breeze, rolls about.
Just as fear seizes a naive girl
If she returns home at night alone.
Thus the drop, shaken in tiny storms,
Now in its virginal shyness fears everything,
Until the engendering sun warms its hovering form

With gentle rays and draws it back to splendor.
Such, if it could be seen in the human flower,
Is the exiled soul, constantly aware of long delays;
It too, thinking of the feasts of its native heaven,
Overturns the drinking cups and purple banquet
      couches.
A drop of the sacred fountain, a glimmer of eternal light,
It is not caught in Tyrian robe or scent of Saba,
But withdrawing completely into the fortress of its
      own light,
It draws inward, closing upon itself.
Conforming in its nature with the arching heaven of
      the great gods,
It builds a starry heaven in its small sphere.
How well contracted into a little image of the heavens,
It shuts up everywhere its side opposed to the world.
But, ornate, it drinks the rays of the sun into its
      rounded mirror,
And shines, open to the surrounding light.
Glowing where it faces the gods, but darker below;
Scorning all else, it burns with love of the heavens.
It leaps up, desiring to depart quickly,
Fully ready, freed for its heavenly journey.
And, its whole surface stretched in aerial course,
Leaving in an instant, it speeds to its goal.
Not otherwise did manna, overflowing with blessed
      nourishment,

Lie, a frozen drop, on the desert soil:
A frozen drop on the ground, but drawn by propitious
    suns,
It returns, purer, to the stars whence it fell.

THE CORONET

When for the Thorns with which I long, too long,
    With many a piercing wound,
    My Saviours head have crown'd,
I seek with Garlands to redress that Wrong;
    Through every Garden, every Mead,
I gather flow'rs (my fruits are only flow'rs)
    Dismantling all the fragrant Towers
That once adorn'd my Shepherdesses head.
And now when I have summ'd up all my store,
    Thinking (so I my self deceive)
    So rich a Chaplet thence to weave
As never yet the king of Glory wore:
    Alas I find the Serpent old
    That, twining in his speckled breast,
    About the flow'rs disguis'd does fold,
    With wreaths of Fame and Interest.
Ah, foolish Man, that would'st debase with them,
And mortal Glory, Heavens Diadem!
But thou who only could'st the Serpent tame,
Either his slipp'ry knots at once untie,
And disintangle all his winding Snare:
Or shatter too with him my curious frame:
And let these wither, so that he may die,
Though set with Skill and chosen out with Care.
That they, while Thou on both their Spoils dost tread,
May crown thy Feet, that could not crown thy Head.

A DIALOGUE BETWEEN THE
SOUL AND BODY

Soul

   O Who shall, from this Dungeon, raise
A Soul enslav'd so many wayes?
With bolts of Bones, that fetter'd stands
In Feet; and manacled in Hands.
Here blinded with an Eye; and there
Deaf with the drumming of an Ear.
A Soul hung up, as 'twere, in Chains
Of Nerves, and Arteries, and Veins.
Tortur'd, besides each other part,
In a vain Head, and double Heart.

Body

   O who shall me deliver whole,
From bonds of this Tyrannic Soul?
Which, stretcht upright, impales me so,
That mine own Precipice I go;
And warms and moves this needless Frame:
(A Fever could but do the same.)
And, wanting where its spight to try,
Has made me live to let me dye.
A Body that could never rest,
Since this ill Spirit it possest.

Soul

    What Magick could me thus confine
Within anothers Grief to pine?
Where whatsoever it complain,
I feel, that cannot feel, the pain.
And all my Care its self employes,
That to preserve, which me destroys:
Constrain'd not only to indure
Diseases, but, whats worse, the Cure:
And ready oft the Port to gain,
Am Shipwrackt into Health again.

Body

    But Physick yet could never reach
The Maladies Thou me dost teach;
Whom first the Cramp of Hope does Tear:
And then the Palsie Shakes of Fear.
The Pestilence of Love does heat:
Or Hatred's hidden Ulcer eat.
Joy's chearful Madness does perplex:
Or Sorrow's other Madness vex.
Which Knowledge forces me to know;
And Memory will not foregoe.
What but a Soul could have the wit
To build me up for Sin so fit?
So Architects do square and hew
Green Trees that in the Forest grew.

A DIALOGUE, BETWEEN THE RESOLVED SOUL, AND CREATED PLEASURE

Courage my Soul, now learn to wield
The weight of thine immortal Shield.
Close on thy Head thy Helmet bright.
Ballance thy Sword against the Fight.
See where an Army, strong as fair,
With silken Banners spreads the air.
Now, if thou bee'st that thing Divine,
In this day's Combat let it shine:
And shew that Nature wants an Art
To conquer one resolved Heart.

Pleasure
Welcome the Creations Guest,
Lord of Earth, and Heavens Heir.
Lay aside that Warlike Crest,
And of Nature's banquet share:
Where the Souls of fruits and flow'rs
Stand prepar'd to heighten yours.

Soul
I sup above, and cannot stay
To bait so long upon the way.

Pleasure
On these downy Pillows lye,
Whose soft Plumes will thither fly:
On these Roses strow'd so plain
Lest one Leaf thy Side should strain.

Soul
My gentler Rest is on a Thought,
Conscious of doing what I ought.

Pleasure
If thou bee'st with Perfumes pleas'd,
Such as oft the Gods appeas'd,
Thou in fragrant Clouds shalt show
Like another God below.

Soul
A Soul that knowes not to presume
Is Heaven's and its own perfume.

Pleasure
Every thing does seem to vie
Which should first attract thine Eye:
But since none deserves that grace,
In this Crystal view *thy* face.

Soul
When the Creator's skill is priz'd,
The rest is all but Earth disguis'd.

Pleasure
Hark how Musick then prepares
For thy Stay these charming Aires;
Which the posting Winds recall,
And suspend the Rivers Fall.

Soul
Had I but any time to lose,
On this I would it all dispose.
Cease Tempter. None can chain a mind
Whom this sweet Chordage cannot bind.

Chorus
Earth cannot shew so brave a Sight
As when a single Soul does fence
The Batteries of alluring Sense,
And Heaven views it with delight.
Then preserve: for still new Charges sound:
And if thou overcom'st thou shalt be crown'd.

Pleasure
All this fair, and soft, and sweet,
   Which scatteringly doth shine,

Shall within one Beauty meet,
    And she be only thine.

Soul
If things of Sight such Heavens be,
What Heavens are those we cannot see?

Pleasure
Where so e're thy Foot shall go
    The minted Gold shall lie,
Till thou purchase all below,
    And want new Worlds to buy.

Soul
Wer't not a price who'ld value Gold?
And that's worth nought that can be sold.

Pleasure
Wilt thou all the Glory have
    That War or Peace commend?
Half the World shall be thy Slave
    The other half thy Friend.

Soul
What Friends, if to my self untrue?
What Slaves, unless I captive you?

Pleasure
Thou shalt know each hidden Cause:
   And see the future Time:
Try what depth the Centre draws;
   And then to Heaven climb.

Soul
None thither mounts by the degree
Of Knowledge, but Humility.

Chorus
Triumph, triumph, victorious Soul;
The World has not one Pleasure more:
The rest does lie beyond the Pole,
And is thine everlasting Store.

OF MOURNING

MOURNING

You, that decipher out the Fate
Of humane Off-springs from the Skies,
What mean these Infants which of late
Spring from the Starrs of *Chlora's* Eyes?

Her Eyes confus'd, and doubled ore,
With Tears suspended ere they flow;
Seem bending upwards, to restore
To Heaven, whence it came, their Woe:

When, molding off the watry Sphears,
Slow drops unty themselves away;
As if she, with those precious Tears,
Would strow the ground where *Strephon* lay.

Yet some affirm, pretending Art,
Her Eyes have so her Bosome drown'd,
Only to soften near her Heart
A place to fix another Wound.

And, while vain Pomp does her restrain
Within her solitary Bowr,
She courts her self in am'rous Rain;
Her self both *Danae* and the Showr.

Nay others, bolder, hence esteem
Joy now so much her Master grown,
That whatsoever does but seem
Like Grief, is from her Windows thrown.

Nor that she payes, while she survives,
To her dead Love this Tribute due;
But casts abroad these Donatives
At the installing of a new.

How wide they dream! The *Indian* Slaves
That sink for Pearl through Seas profound,
Would find her Tears yet deeper Waves
And not of one the bottom sound.

I yet my silent Judgment keep,
Disputing not what they believe:
But sure as oft as Women weep,
It is to be suppos'd they grieve.

THE NYMPH COMPLAINING FOR
THE DEATH OF HER FAUN

The wanton Troopers riding by
Have shot my Faun and it will dye.
Ungentle men! They cannot thrive
To kill thee. Thou neer didst alive
Them any harm: alas nor cou'd
Thy death yet do them any good.
I'me sure I never wisht them ill;
Nor do I for all this; nor will:
But, if my simple Pray'rs may yet
Prevail with Heaven to forget
Thy murder, I will Joyn my Tears
Rather than fail. But, O my fears!
It cannot dye so. Heavens King
Keeps register of every thing:
And nothing may we use in vain.
Ev'n Beasts must be with justice slain;
Else Men are made their *Deodands.*
Though they should wash their guilty hands
In this warm life-blood, which doth part
From thine, and wound me to the Heart,
Yet could they not be clean: their Stain
Is dy'd in such a Purple Grain.
There is not such another in
The World, to offer for their Sin.

Unconstant *Sylvio*, when yet
I had not found him counterfeit,
One morning (I remember well)
Ty'd in this silver Chain and Bell,
Gave it to me: nay and I know
What he said then; I'me sure I do.
Said He, look how your Huntsman here
Hath taught a Faun to hunt his *Dear*.
But *Sylvio* soon had me beguil'd.
This waxed tame, while he grew wild,
And quite regardless of my Smart,
Left me his Faun, but took his Heart.

Thenceforth I set my self to play
My solitary time away,
With this: and very well content,
Could so mine idle Life have spent.
For it was full of sport; and light
Of foot, and heart; and did invite,
Me to its game: it seem'd to bless
Its self in me. How could I less
Than love it? O I cannot be
Unkind, t' a Beast that loveth me.

Had it liv'd long, I do not know
Whether it too might have done so
As *Sylvio* did: his Gifts might be
Perhaps as false or more than he.
But I am sure, for ought that I

Could in so short a time espie,
Thy Love was far more better then
The love of false and cruel men.

 With sweetest milk, and sugar, first
I it at mine own fingers nurst.
And as it grew, so every day
It wax'd more white and sweet than they.
It had so sweet a Breath! And oft
I blush to see its foot more soft,
And white, (shall I say then my hand?)
Nay, any Ladies of the Land.

 It is a wond'rous thing, how fleet
'Twas on those little silver feet.
With what a pretty skipping grace,
It oft would challenge me the Race:
And when 't had left me far away,
'Twould stay, and run again, and stay.
For it was nimbler much than Hindes;
And trod, as on the four Winds.

 I have a Garden of my own,
But so with Roses over grown,
And Lillies, that you would it guess
To be a little Wilderness.
And all the Spring time of the year
It onely loved to be there.
Among the beds of Lillyes, I
Have sought it oft, where it should lye;

Yet could not, till it self would rise,
Find it, although before mine Eyes.
For, in the flaxen Lillies shade,
It like a bank of Lillies laid.
Upon the Roses it would feed,
Until its Lips ev'n seem'd to bleed:
And then to me 'twould boldly trip,
And print those Roses on my Lip.
But all its chief delight was still
On Roses thus its self to fill:
And its pure virgin Limbs to fold
In whitest sheets of Lillies cold.
Had it liv'd long, it would have been
Lillies without, Roses within.

 O help! O help! I see it faint:
And dye as calmely as a Saint.
See how it weeps. The Tears do come
Sad, slowly dropping like a Gumme.
So weeps the wounded Balsome: so
The holy Frankincense doth flow.
The brotherless *Heliades*
Melt in such Amber Tears as these.

 I in a golden Vial will
Keep these two crystal Tears; and fill
It till it do o'reflow with mine;
Then place it in *Diana's* Shrine.

 Now my sweet Faun is vanish'd to

Whither the Swans and Turtles go:
In fair *Elizium* to endure,
With milk-white Lambs, and Ermins pure.
O do not run too fast: for I
Will but bespeak thy Grave, and dye.
   First my unhappy Statue shall
But cut in Marble; and withal,
Let it be weeping too: but there
Th' Engraver sure his Art may spare;
For I so truly thee bemoane,
That I shall weep though I be Stone:
Until my Tears, still dropping, wear
My breast, themselves engraving there.
There at my feet shalt thou be laid,
Of purest Alabaster made:
For I would have thine Image be
White as I can, though not as Thee.

UPON THE DEATH OF THE
LORD *HASTINGS*

Go, intercept some Fountain in the Vein,
Whose Virgin-Source yet never steept the Plain.
Hastings is dead, and we must finde a Store
Of Tears untoucht, and never wept before.
Go, stand betwixt the *Morning* and the *Flowers*;
And, ere they fall, arrest the early *Showers*.
Hastings is dead; and we, disconsolate,
With early *Tears* must mourn his early *Fate*.
   Alas, his *Vertues* did his *Death* presage:
Needs must he die, that doth out-run his *Age*.
The Phlegmatick and Slowe prolongs his day,
And on Times Wheel sticks like a *Remora*.
What man is he, that hath no *Heaven* beguil'd,
And is not thence mistaken for a *Childe*?
While those of growth more sudden, and more bold,
Are hurried hence, as if already old.
For, there above, They number not as here,
But weigh to Man the *Geometrick* yeer.
   Had he but at this Measure still increast,
And on *the Tree of Life* once made a Feast,
As that of *Knowledge*; what Loves had he given
To Earth, and then what Jealousies to Heaven!
But 'tis a *Maxime* of that State, That none,
Lest He becomes like Them, taste more than one.

Therefore the *Democratick* Stars did rise,
And all that Worth from hence did *Ostracize*.

Yet as some *Prince*, that, for State-Jealousie,
Secures his neerest and most lov'd *Ally*;
His Thought with richest Triumphs entertains,
And in the choicest Pleasures charms his Pains:
So he, not banisht hence, but there confin'd,
There better recreates his active Minde.

Before the *Chrystal Palace* where he dwells,
The armed *Angels* hold their *Carouzels*;
And underneath, he views the *Turnaments*
Of all these Sublunary *Elements*.
But most he doth th' *Eternal Book* behold,
On which the *happie Names* do stand enroll'd;
And gladly there can all his Kindred claim,
But most rejoyces at his *Mothers* name.

The gods themselves cannot their Joy conceal,
But draw their Veils, and their pure Beams reveal:
Onely they drooping *Hymeneus* note,
Who for sad *Purple*, tears his *Saffron*-coat;
And trails his Torches th'row the Starry Hall
Reversed, at his *Darlings* Funeral.

And *Æsculapius*, who, asham'd and stern,
Himself at once condemneth, and *Mayern*;

89

Like some sad *Chymist*, who prepar'd to reap
The *Golden Harvest*, sees his Glasses leap.
For, how Immortal must their Race have stood,
Had *Mayern* once been mixt wth *Hastings* blood!
How Sweet and Verdant would these *Lawrels* be,
Had they been planted on that *Balsam*-tree!

   But what could he, good man, although he bruis'd
All Herbs, and them a thousand ways infus'd?
All he had try'd, but all in vain, he saw,
And wept, as we, without Redress or Law.
For *Man* (alas) is but the *Heavens* sport;
And *Art* indeed is Long, but *Life* is Short.

TOM MAY'S DEATH

As one put drunk into the Packet-boat,
Tom May was hurry'd hence and did not know't.
But was amaz'd on the Elysian side,
And with an Eye uncertain, gazing wide,
Could not determine in what place he was,
For whence in Stevens ally Trees or Grass.
Nor where the Popes head, nor the Mitre lay,
Signs by which still he found and lost his way.
At last while doubtfully he all compares,
He saw near hand, as he imagin'd *Ares*.
Such did he seem for corpulence and port,
But 'twas a man much of another sort;
'Twas *Ben* that in the dusky Laurel shade
Amongst the Chorus of old Poets laid,
Sounding of ancient Heroes, such as were
The Subjects Safety, and the Rebel's Fear,
But how a double headed Vulture Eats
Brutus and *Cassius*, the Peoples cheats.
But seeing *May* he varied streight his Song,
Gently to signifie that he was wrong.
Cups more than civil of *Emathian* wine,
I sing (said he) and the *Pharsalian* Sign,
Where the Historian of the Common-wealth
In his own Bowels sheath'd the conquering health.
By this *May* to himself and them was come,

He found he was translated, and by whom.
Yet then with foot as stumbling as his tongue
Prest for his place among the Learned throng.
But *Ben*, who knew not neither foe nor friend,
Sworn Enemy to all that do pretend,
Rose more than ever he was seen severe,
Shook his gray locks, and his own Bayes did tear
At this intrusion. Then with Laurel wand,
The awful Sign of his supream command,
At whose dread Whisk *Virgil* himself does quake,
And *Horace* patiently its stroke does take,
As he crowds in he whipt him ore the pate
Like *Pembroke* at the Masque, and then did rate:

    "Far from these blessed shades tread back agen
Most servil wit, and Mercenary Pen.
Polydore, Lucan, Allan, Vandale, Goth,
Malignant Poet and Historian both.
Go seek the novice Statesmen, and obtrude
On them some Romane cast similitude,
Tell them of Liberty, the Stories fine,
Until you all grow Consuls in your wine.
Or thou *Dictator* of the glass bestow
On him the *Cato*, this the *Cicero*.
Transferring old *Rome* hither in your talk,
As *Bethlem's* House did to *Loretto* walk.
Foul Architect that hadst not Eye to see
How ill the measures of these States agree.

And who by *Romes* example *England* lay,
Those but to *Lucan* do continue *May*.
But thee nor Ignorance nor seeming good
Misled, but malice fixt and understood.
Because some one than thee more worthy weares
The sacred Laurel, hence are all these tears?
Must therefore all the World be set on flame,
Because a Gazet writer mist his aim?
And for a Tankard-bearing Muse must we
As for the Basket *Guelphs* and *Gibellines* be?
When the Sword glitters ore the Judges head,
And fear has Coward Churchmen silenced,
Then is the Poets time, 'tis then he drawes,
And single fights forsaken Vertues cause.
He, when the wheel of Empire, whirleth back,
And though the World's disjointed Axel crack,
Sings still of ancient Rights and better Times,
Seeks wretched good, arraigns successful Crimes.
But thou base man first prostituted hast
Our spotless knowledge and the studies chaste,
Apostatizing from our Arts and us,
To turn the Chronicler to *Spartacus*.
Yet wast thou taken hence with equal fate,
Before thou couldst great *Charles* his death relate.
But what will deeper wound thy little mind,
Hast left surviving *Davenant* still behind
Who laughs to see in this thy death renew'd,

Right Romane poverty and gratitude.
Poor Poet thou, and grateful Senate they,
Who thy last Reckoning did so largely pay.
And with the publick gravity would come,
When thou hadst drunk thy last to lead thee home.
If that can be thy home where *Spencer* lyes
And reverend *Chaucer*, but their dust does rise
Against thee, and expels thee from their side,
As th' Eagles Plumes from other birds divide.
Nor here thy shade must dwell; Return, Return,
Where Sulphrey *Phlegeton* does ever burn.
Thee *Cerberus* with all his Jawes shall gnash,
Megæra thee with all her Serpents lash.
Thou rivited unto *Ixion's* wheel
Shalt break, and the perpetual Vulture feel.
'Tis just what Torments Poets ere did feign,
Thou first Historically shouldst sustain."

    Thus by irrevocable Sentence cast,
    May only Master of these Revels past.
    And streight he vanisht in a Cloud of pitch,
    Such as unto the Sabboth bears the Witch.

THE SECOND CHORUS FROM
SENECA'S TRAGEDY, *THYESTES*

Stet quicunque volet potens
Aulae culmine lubrico etc.

TRANSLATION

Climb at *Court* for me that will
Tottering Favour's slipp'ry hill.
All I seek is to lye still.
Settled in some secret Nest
In calm Leisure let me rest;
And far off the publick Stage
Pass away my silent Age.
Thus when without noise, unknown,
I have liv'd out all my span,
I shall dye, without a groan,
An old honest Country man.
Who expos'd to others Eyes,
Into his own Heart ne'r pry's,
Death to him's a Strange surprise.

OF LANDSCAPE AND
ARCHITECTURE

UPON THE HILL AND GROVE AT
BILL-BOROW
To the Lord *Fairfax*

See how the arched Earth does here
Rise in a perfect Hemisphere!
The stiffest Compass could not strike
A Line more circular and like;
Nor softest Pensel draw a Brow
So equal as this Hill does bow.
It seems as for a Model laid,
And that the World by it was made.

Here learn ye Mountains more unjust,
Which to abrupter greatness thrust,
That do with your hook-shoulder'd height
The Earth deform and Heaven fright.
For whose excrescence ill design'd,
Nature must a new Center find,
Learn here those humble steps to tread,
Which to securer Glory lead.

See what a soft access and wide
Lyes open to its grassy side;
Nor with the rugged path deterrs
The feet of breathless Travellers.
See then how courteous it ascends,
And all the way it rises bends;
Nor for it self the height does gain,
But only strives to raise the Plain.

Yet thus it all the field commands,
And in unenvy'd Greatness stands,
Discerning further than the Cliff
Of Heaven-daring *Teneriff.*
How glad the weary Seamen hast
When they salute it from the Mast!
By Night the Northern Star their way
Directs, and this no less by Day.

Upon its crest this Mountain grave
A Plump of aged Trees does wave.
No hostile hand durst ere invade
With impious Steel the sacred Shade.
For something alwaies did appear
Of the *great Master's* terrour there:
And Men could hear his Armour still
Ratling through all the Grove and Hill.

Fear of the *Master*, and respect
Of the great *Nymph* did it protect;
Vera the *Nymph* that him inspir'd,
To whom he often here retir'd,
And on these Okes ingrav'd her Name;
Such Wounds alone these Woods became:
But ere he well the Barks could part
'Twas writ already in their Heart.

For they ('tis credible) have sense,
As We, of Love and Reverence,
And underneath the Courser Rind
The *Genius* of the house do bind.
Hence they successes seem to know,
And in their *Lord's* advancement grow;
But in no Memory were seen
As under this so streight and green.

Yet now no further strive to shoot,
Contented if they fix their Root.
Nor to the wind's uncertain gust,
Their prudent Heads too far intrust.
Onely sometimes a flutt'ring Breez
Discourses with the breathing Trees;
Which in their modest Whispers name
Those Acts that swell'd the Cheek of Fame.

Much other Groves, say they, than these
And other Hills him once did please.
Through Groves of Pikes he thunder'd then,
And Mountains rais'd of dying Men.
For all the *Civick Garlands* due
To him our Branches are but few.
Nor are our Trunks enow to bear
The *Trophees* of one fertile Year.

'Tis true, yee Trees, nor ever spoke
More certain *Oracles* in Oak.
But Peace (if you his favour prize),
That Courage its own Praises flies.
Therefore to your obscurer Seats
From his own Brightness he retreats:
Nor he the Hills without the Groves,
Nor Height but with Retirement loves.

UPON *APPLETON* HOUSE
To my Lord *Fairfax*

Within this sober Frame expect
Work of no Forrain *Architect*;
That unto Caves the Quarries drew,
And Forrests did to Pastures hew;
Who of his great Design in pain
Did for a Model vault his Brain,
Whose Columnes should so high be rais'd
To arch the Brows that on them gaz'd.

Why should of all things Man unrul'd
Such unproportion'd dwellings build?
The Beasts are by their Denns exprest:
And Birds contrive an equal Nest;
The low roof'd Tortoises do dwell
In cases fit of Tortoise-shell:
No Creature loves an empty space;
Their Bodies measure out their Place.

But He, superfluously spread,
Demands more room alive than dead.
And in his hollow Palace goes
Where Winds (as he) themselves may lose.
What need of all this Marble Crust
T'impark the wanton Mote of Dust,
That thinks by Breadth the World t'unite
Though the first Builders fail'd in Height?

But all things are composed here
Like Nature, orderly and near:
In which we the Dimensions find
Of that more sober Age and Mind,
When larger-sized Men did stoop
To enter at a narrow loop;
As practising, in doors so strait,
To strain themselves through *Heavens Gate*.

And surely when the after Age
Shall hither come in *Pilgrimage*,
These sacred Places to adore,
By *Vere* and *Fairfax* trod before,
Men will dispute how their Extent
Within such dwarfish Confines went:
And some will smile at this, as well
As *Romulus* his Bee-like Cell.

Humility alone designs
Those short but admirable Lines,
By which, ungirt and unconstrain'd,
Things greater are in less contain'd.
Let others vainly strive t'immure
The Circle in the *Quadrature*!
These *holy Mathematicks* can
In ev'ry Figure equal Man.

Yet thus the laden horse does sweat,
And scarce indures the *Master* great:
But where he comes the swelling Hall
Stirs, and the *Square* grows *Spherical*;
More by his *Magnitude* distrest,
Than he is by its straitness prest:
And too officiously it slights
That in it self which him delights.

So Honour better Lowness bears,
Than That unwonted Greatness wears.
Height with a certain Grace does bend,
But low Things clownishly ascend.
And yet what needs there here Excuse,
Where evry Thing does answer Use?
Where neatness nothing can condemn,
Nor Pride invent what to contemn?

A Stately *Frontispice of Poor*
Adorns without the open Door:
Nor less the Rooms within commends
Daily new *Furniture of Friends*.
The House was built upon the Place
Only as for a *Mark of Grace*;
And for an *Inn* to entertain
Its *Lord* a while, but not remain.

Him *Bishops-Hill*, or *Denton* may,
Or *Bilbrough*, better hold than they:
But Nature here hath been so free
As if she said leave this to me.
Art would more neatly have defac'd
What she had laid so sweetly waste;
In fragrant Gardens, shady Woods,
Deep Meadows, and transparent Floods.

While with slow Eyes we these survey,
And on each pleasant footstep stay,
We opportunly may relate
The Progress of this Houses Fate.
A *Nunnery* first gave it birth.
For *Virgin-Buildings* oft brought forth.
And all that Neighbour-Ruine shows
The Quarries whence this dwelling rose.

Near to this gloomy Cloysters Gates
There dwelt the blooming Virgin *Thwates*,
Fair beyond Measure, and an Heir
Which might Deformity make fair.
And oft She spent the Summer Suns
Discoursing with the *Suttle Nunns*.
Whence in these Words one to her weav'd,
(As 'twere by Chance) Thoughts long conceiv'd.

"Within this holy leisure we
Live innocently as you see.
These Walls restrain the World without,
But hedge our Liberty about.
These Bars inclose that wider Den
Of those wild Creatures, called Men.
The Cloyster outward shuts its Gates,
And, from us, locks on them the Grates.

"Here we, in shining Armour white,
Like *Virgin-Amazons* do fight.
And our chaste *Lamps* we hourly trim,
Lest the great *Bridegroom* find them dim.
Our *Orient* Breaths perfumed are
With incense of incessant Pray'r.
And Holy-water of our Tears
Most strangely our Complexion clears.

"Not Tears of Grief; but such as those
With which calm Pleasure overflows;
Or Pity, when we look on you
That live without this happy Vow.
How should we grieve that must be seen
Each one a *Spouse*, and each a *Queen*;
And can in *Heaven* hence behold
Our brighter Robes and Crowns of Gold?

"When we have prayed all our Beads,
Some One the holy *Legend* reads;
While all the rest with Needles paint
The Face and Graces of the *Saint*.
But what the Linnen can't receive
They in their Lives do interweave.
This Work the *Saints* best represents;
That serves for *Altar's Ornaments*.

"But much it to our work would add
If here your hand, your Face we had:
By it we would *our Lady* touch;
Yet thus She you resembles much.
Some of your Features, as we sow'd,
Through ev'ry *Shrine* should be bestow'd.
And in one Beauty we would take
Enough a thousand *Saints* to make.

"And (for I dare not quench the Fire
That me does for your good inspire)
'Twere Sacriledge a Man t'admit
To holy things, for *Heaven* fit.
I see the *Angels* in a Crown
On you the Lillies show'ring down:
And round about your Glory breaks,
That something more than humane speaks.

"All Beauty, when at such a height,
Is so already consecrate.
Fairfax I know; and long ere this
Have mark'd the Youth, and what he is.
But can he such a *Rival* seem
For whom you Heav'n should disesteem?
Ah, no! and 'twould more Honour prove
He your *Devoto* were, than *Love*.

"Here live beloved, and obey'd:
Each one your Sister, each your Maid.
And, if our Rule seem strictly pend,
The Rule it self to you shall bend.
Our *Abbess* too, now far in Age,
Doth your succession near presage.
How soft the yoke on us would lye,
Might such fair Hands as yours it tye!

"Your voice, the sweetest of the Quire,
Shall draw *Heav'n* nearer, raise us higher.
And your Example, if our Head,
Will soon us to perfection lead.
Those Virtues to us all so dear,
Will straight grow Sanctity when here:
And that, once sprung, increase so fast
Till Miracles it work at last.

"Nor is our *Order* yet so nice,
Delight to banish as a Vice.
Here Pleasure Piety doth meet;
One perfecting the other Sweet.
So through the mortal fruit we boyl
The Sugars uncorrupting Oyl:
And that which perisht while we pull,
Is thus preserved clear and full.

"For such indeed are all our Arts;
Still handling Natures finest Parts.
Flow'rs dress the Altars; for the Clothes,
The Sea-Born Amber we compose;
Balms for the griev'd we draw; and Pastes
We mold, as Baits for curious tastes.
What need is here of Man? unless
These as sweet Sins we should confess.

"Each Night among us to your side
Appoint a fresh and Virgin Bride;
Whom if *our Lord* at midnight find,
Yet Neither should be left behind.
Where you may lye as chaste in Bed,
As Pearls together billeted.
All Night embracing Arm in Arm,
Like Chrystal pure with Cotton warm.

"But what is this to all the store
Of Joys you see, and may make more!
Try but a while, if you be wise:
The Tryal neither Costs, nor Tyes."
Now *Fairfax* seek her promis'd faith:
Religion that dispensed hath,
Which She hence forward does begin;
The *Nuns* smooth Tongue has suckt her in.

Oft, though he knew it was in vain,
Yet would he valiantly complain.
"Is this that *Sanctity* so great,
An Art by which you finly'r cheat?
Hypocrite Witches, hence *avant*,
Who though in prison yet inchant!
Death only can such Theeves make fast,
As rob though in the Dungeon cast.

"Were there but, when this House was made,
One Stone that a just Hand had laid,
It must have fall'n upon her Head
Who first Thee from thy Faith misled.
And yet, how well soever ment,
With them 'twould soon grow fraudulent,
For like themselves they alter all,
And vice infects the very Wall.

"But sure those Buildings last not long,
Founded by Folly, kept by Wrong.
I know what Fruit their Gardens yield,
When they it think by Night conceal'd.
Fly from their Vices. 'Tis thy 'state,
Not Thee, that they would consecrate.
Fly from their Ruine. How I fear,
Though guiltless, lest thou perish there."

What should he do? He would respect
Religion, but not Right neglect:
For first Religion taught him Right,
And dazled not but clear'd his sight.
Sometimes resolv'd his Sword he draws,
But reverenceth then the Laws:
For Justice still that Courage led;
First from a Judge, then Souldier bred.

Small Honour would be in the Storm.
The *Court* him grants the lawful Form;
Which licens'd either Peace or Force,
To hinder the unjust Divorce.
Yet still the *Nuns* his Right debar'd,
Standing upon their holy Guard.
Ill-counsell'd Women, do you know
Whom you resist, or what you do?

Is not this he whose Offspring fierce
Shall fight through all the *Universe*;
And with successive Valour try
France, *Poland*, either *Germany*;
Till one, as long since prophecy'd,
His Horse through conquer'd *Britain* ride?
Yet, against Fate, his Spouse they kept;
And the great Race would intercept.

Some to the Breach against their Foes
Their *Wooden Saints* in vain oppose.
Another bolder stands at push
With their old *Holy-Water Brush*.
While the disjointed *Abbess* threads
The gingling Chain-shot of her *Beads*.
But their lowd'st Cannon were their Lungs;
And sharpest Weapons were their Tongues.

But, waving these aside like Flyes,
Young *Fairfax* through the Wall does rise.
Then th' unfrequented Vault appear'd,
And superstitions vainly feard.
The *Relicks false* were set to view;
Only the Jewels there were true:
But truly bright and holy *Thwaites*
That weeping at the *Altar* waites.

But the glad Youth away her bears,
And to the *Nuns* bequeaths her Tears:
Who guiltily their Prize bemoan,
Like Gipsies that a child had stoln.
Thenceforth (as when th' Inchantment ends
The Castle vanishes or rends)
The wasting Cloister with the rest
Was in one instant dispossest.

At the demolishing, this Seat
To *Fairfax* fell as by Escheat.
And what both *Nuns* and *Founders* will'd
'Tis likely better thus fulfill'd.
For if the *Virgin* prov'd not theirs,
The *Cloyster* yet remained hers.
Though many a *Nun* there made her Vow,
'Twas no *Religious House* till now.

From that blest Bed the *Heroe* came,
Whom *France* and *Poland* yet does fame:
Who, when retired here to Peace,
His warlike Studies could not cease;
But laid these Gardens out in sport
In the just Figure of a Fort;
And with five Bastions it did fence,
As aiming one for ev'ry Sense.

When in the *East* the Morning Ray
Hangs out the Colours of the Day,
The Bee through these known Allies hums,
Beating the *Dian* with its *Drumms.*
Then Flow'rs their drowsie Eylids raise,
Their Silken Ensigns each displayes,
And dries its Pan yet dank with Dew,
And fills its Flask with Odours new.

These, as their *Governour* goes by,
In fragrant Vollyes they let fly;
And to salute their *Governess*
Again as great a charge they press:
None for the *Virgin Nymph*; for She
Seems with the Flow'rs a Flow'r to be.
And think so still! though not compare
With Breath so sweet, or Cheek so faire.

Well shot ye Firemen! Oh how sweet,
And round your equal Fires do meet;
Whose shrill report no Ear can tell,
But Ecchoes to the Eye and smell.
See how the Flow'rs, as at *Parade*,
Under their *Colours* stand displaid:
Each *Regiment* in order grows,
That of the Tulip, Pinke, and Rose.

But when the vigilant *Patroul*
Of Stars walks round about the *Pole*,
Their Leaves, that to the stalks are curl'd,
Seem to their Staves the *Ensigns* furl'd.
Then in some Flow'rs beloved Hut
Each Bee as Sentinel is shut;
And sleeps so too: but, if once stir'd,
She runs you through, nor askes *the Word*.

Oh Thou, that dear and happy Isle
The Garden of the World ere while,
Thou *Paradise* of four Seas,
Which *Heaven* planted us to please,
But, to exclude the World, did guard
With watry if not flaming Sword;
What luckless Apple did we taste,
To make us Mortal, and Thee Waste?

Unhappy! shall we never more
That sweet *Militia* restore,
When Gardens only had their Towrs,
And all the Garrisons were Flowrs,
When Roses only Arms might bear,
And Men did rosie Garlands wear?
Tulips, in several Colours barr'd,
Were then the *Switzers* of our *Guard*.

The *Gardiner* had the *Souldiers* place,
And his more gentle Forts did trace.
The Nursery of all things green
Was then the only *Magazeen*.
The *Winter Quarters* were the Stoves,
Where he the tender Plants removes.
But War all this doth overgrow:
We Ord'nance Plant and Powder sow.

And yet there walks one on the Sod
Who, had it pleased him and *God*,
Might once have made our Gardens spring
Fresh as his own and flourishing.
But he preferr'd to the *Cinque Ports*
These five imaginary Forts:
And, in those half-dry Trenches, spann'd
Pow'r which the Ocean might command.

For he did, with his utmost Skill,
Ambition weed, but *Conscience* till.
Conscience, that Heaven-nursed Plant,
Which most our Earthly Gardens want.
A prickling leaf it bears, and such
As that which shrinks at ev'ry touch;
But Flowrs eternal, and divine,
That in the Crowns of Saints do shine.

The sight does from these *Bastions* ply,
Th' invisible *Artilery*;
And at proud *Cawood-Castle* seems
To point the *Battery* of its Beams.
As if it quarrell'd in the Seat
Th' Ambition of its *Prelate* great.
But ore the Meads below it plays,
Or innocently seems to gaze.

And now to the Abbyss I pass
Of that unfathomable Grass,
Where Men like Grashoppers appear,
But Grashoppers are Gyants there:
They, in there squeaking Laugh, contemn
Us as we walk more low than them:
And, from the Precipices tall
Of the green spires, to us do call.

To see Men through this Meadow Dive,
We wonder how they rise alive.
As, under Water, none does know
Whether he fall through it or go.
But, as the Marriners that sound,
And show upon their Lead the Ground,
They bring up Flow'rs so to be seen,
And prove they've at the Bottom been.

No Scene that turns with Engines strange
Does oftner than these Meadows change.
For when the Sun the Grass hath vext,
The tawny Mowers enter next;
Who seem like *Israelites* to be,
Walking on foot through a green Sea.
To them the Grassy Deeps divide,
And crowd a Lane to either Side.

With whistling Sithe, and Elbow strong,
These Massacre the Grass along:
While one, unknowing, carves the *Rail*,
Whose yet unfeather'd Quils her fail.
The Edge all bloody from its Breast
He draws, and does his stroke detest;
Fearing the Flesh untimely mow'd
To him a Fate as black forebode.

But bloody *Thestylis*, that waites
To bring the mowing Camp their Cates,
Greedy as Kites has trust it up,
And forthwith means on it to sup:
When on another quick She lights,
And cryes, "He call'd us *Israelites*;
But now, to make his saying true,
Rails rain for Quails, for Manna Dew."

Unhappy Birds! what does it boot
To build below the Grasses Root;
When Lowness is unsafe as Hight,
And Chance o'retakes what scapeth spight?
And now your Orphan Parents Call
Sounds your untimely Funeral.
Death Trumpets creak in such a Note,
And 'tis the *Sourdine* in their Throat.

Or sooner hatch or higher build:
The Mower now commands the Field;
In whose new Traverse seemeth wrought
A Camp of Battail newly fought:
Where, as the Meads with Hay, the Plain
Lyes quilted ore with Bodies slain:
The Women that with forks it fling,
Do represent the Pillaging.

And now the careless Victors play,
Dancing the Triumphs of the Hay;
Where every Mowers wholesome Heat
Smells like an *Alexanders sweat*.
Their Females fragrant as the Mead
Which they in *Fairy Circles* tread:
When at their Dances End they kiss,
Their new-made Hay not sweeter is.

When after this 'tis pil'd in Cocks,
Like a calm Sea it shews the Rocks:
We wondring in the River near
How Boats among them safely steer.
Or, like the *Desert Memphis Sand*,
Short *Pyramids* of Hay do stand.
And such the *Roman Camps* do rise
In Hills for Soldiers Obsequies.

This *Scene* again withdrawing brings
A new and empty Face of things;
A levell'd space, as smooth and plain,
As Clothes for *Lilly* strecht to stain.
The World when first created sure
Was such a Table rase and pure.
Or rather such is the *Toril*
Ere the Bulls enter at Madril.

For to this naked equal Flat,
Which *Levellers* take Pattern at,
The Villagers in common chase
Their Cattle, which it closer rase;
And what below the Scythe increast
Is pincht yet nearer by the Beast.
Such, in the painted World, appear'd
Davenant with th' Universal Heard.

They seem within the polisht Grass
A Landskip drawen in Looking-Glass.
And shrunk in the huge Pasture show
As Spots, so shap'd, on Faces do,
Such Fleas, ere they approach the Eye,
In Multiplying Glasses lye.
They feed so wide, so slowly move,
As *Constellations* do above.

Then, to conclude these pleasant Acts,
Denton sets ope its *Cataracts*;
And makes the Meadow truly be
(What it but seem'd before) a Sea.
For, jealous of its *Lords* long stay,
It try's t'invite him thus away.
The River in it self is drown'd,
And Isles th' astonisht Cattle round.

Let others tell the *Paradox*,
How Eels now bellow in the Ox;
How Horses at their Tails do kick,
Turn'd as they hang to Leeches quick;
How Boats can over Bridges sail;
And Fishes do the Stables scale.
How *Salmons* trespassing are found;
And Pikes are taken in the Pound.

But I, retiring from the Flood,
Take Sanctuary in the Wood;
And, while it lasts, my self imbark
In this yet green, yet growing Ark;
Where the first Carpenter might best
Fit Timber for his Keel have Prest.
And where all Creatures might have shares,
Although in Armies, not in Paires.

The double Wood of ancient Stocks
Link'd in so thick, an Union locks,
It like two *Pedigrees* appears,
On one hand *Fairfax*, th' other *Veres*:
Of whom though many fell in War,
Yet more to Heaven shooting are:
And, as they Natures Cradle deckt,
Will in green Age her Hearse expect.

When first the Eye this Forrest sees
It seems indeed as *Wood* not *Trees*:
As if their Neighbourhood so old
To one great Trunk them all did mold.
There the huge Bulk takes place, as ment
To thrust up a *Fifth Element*;
And stretches still so closely wedg'd
As if the Night within were hedg'd.

Dark all without it knits; within
It opens passable and thin;
And in as loose an order grows,
As the *Corinthean Porticoes*.
The arching Boughs unite between
The Columnes of the Temple green;
And underneath the winged Quires
Echo about their tuned Fires.

The *Nightingale* does here make choice
To sing the Tryals of her Voice.
Low Shrubs she sits in, and adorns
With Musick high the squatted Thorns.
But highest Oakes stoop down to hear,
And listning Elders prick the Ear.
The Thorn, lest it should hurt her, draws
Within the Skin its shrunken claws.

But I have for my Musick found
A Sadder, yet more pleasing Sound:
The *Stock-doves*, whose fair necks are grac'd
With Nuptial Rings their Ensigns chast;
Yet always, for some Cause unknown,
Sad pair unto the Elms they moan.
O why should such a Couple mourn,
That in so equal Flames do burn!

Then, as I carless on the Bed
Of gelid *Straw-berryes* do tread,
And through the Hazles thick espy
The hatching *Thrastle's* shining Eye,
The *Heron* from the Ashes top,
The eldest of its young lets drop,
As if it Stork-like did pretend
That *Tribune* to *its Lord* to send.

But most the *Hewel's* wonders are,
Who here has the *Holt-felsters* care.
He walks still upright from the Root
Meas'ring the Timber with his Foot;
And all the way, to keep it clean,
Doth from the Bark the Wood-moths glean.
He, with his Beak, examines well
Which fit to stand and which to fell.

The good he numbers up, and hacks;
As if he mark'd them with the Ax.
But where he, tinkling with his Beak,
Does find the hollow Oak to speak,
That for his building he designs,
And through the tainted Side he mines.
Who could have thought the *tallest Oak*
Should fall by such a *feeble Stroke*!

Nor would it, had the Tree not fed
A *Traitor-Worm*, within it bred.
(As first our *Flesh* corrupt within
Tempts impotent and bashful *Sin*.)
And yet that *Worm* triumphs not long,
But serves to feed the *Hewels young*.
While the Oake seems to fall content,
Viewing the Treason's Punishment.

Thus I, *easie Philosopher*,
Among the *Birds* and *Trees* confer:
And little now to make me, wants
Or of the *Fowles*, or of the *Plants*.
Give me but Wings as they, and I
Streight floting on the Air shall fly:
Or turn me but, and you shall see
I was but an inverted Tree.

Already I begin to call
In their most learn'd Original:
And where I Language want, my Signs
The Bird upon the Bough divines;
And more attentive there doth sit
Than if She were with Lime-twigs knit.
No Leaf does tremble in the Wind
Which I returning cannot find.

Out of these scatter'd *Sibyls* Leaves
Strange *Prophecies* my Phancy weaves:
And in one History consumes,
Like *Mexique-Paintings*, all the *Plumes*.
What *Rome, Greece, Palestine*, ere said
I in this light *Mosaick* read.
Thrice happy he who, not mistook,
Hath read in *Natures mystick Book*.

And see how Chance's better Wit
Could with a Mask my studies hit!
The Oak-Leaves me embroyder all,
Between which Caterpillars crawl:
And Ivy, with familiar trails,
Me licks, and clasps, and curles, and hales.
Under this *antick Cope* I move
Like some great *Prelate of the Grove*,

Then, languishing with ease, I toss
On Pallets swoln of Velvet Moss;
While the Wind, cooling through the Boughs,
Flatters with Air my panting Brows.
Thanks for my Rest ye *Mossy Banks*,
And unto you *cool Zephyr's* Thanks,
Who, as my Hair, my Thoughts too shed,
And winnow from the Chaff my Head.

How safe, methinks, and strong, behind
These Trees have I incamp'd my Mind;
Where Beauty, aiming at the Heart,
Bends in some Tree its useless Dart;
And where the World no certain Shot
Can make, or me it toucheth not.
But I on it securely play,
And gaul its Horsemen all the Day.

Bind me ye *Woodbines* in your twines,
Curle me about ye gadding *Vines*,
And Oh so close your Circles lace,
That I may never leave this Place:
But, lest your Fetters prove too weak,
Ere I your Silken Bondage break,
Do you, *O Brambles*, chain me too,
And courteous *Briars* nail me through.

Here in the Morning tye my Chain,
Where the two Woods have made a Lane;
While, like a *Guard* on either side,
The Trees before their *Lord* divide:
This, like a long and equal Thread,
Betwixt two *Labyrinths* does lead.
But, where the Floods did lately drown,
There at the Ev'ning stake me down.

For now the Waves are fal'n and dry'd,
And now the Meadow's fresher dy'd;
Whose Grass, with moister colour dasht,
Seems as green Silks but newly washt.
No *Serpent* new nor *Crocodile*
Remains behind our little *Nile*,
Unless it self you will mistake,
Among these Meads the only Snake.

See in what wanton harmless folds
It ev'ry where the Meadow holds;
And its yet muddy back doth lick,
Till as a *Chrystal Mirrour* slick;
Where all things gaze themselves, and doubt
If they be in it or without.
And for his shade which therein shines,
Narcissus like, the *Sun* too pines.

Oh what a Pleasure 'tis to hedge
My Temples here with heavy sedge;
Abandoning my lazy Side,
Stretcht as a Bank unto the Tide;
Or to suspend my sliding Foot
On the Osiers undermined Root,
And in its Branches tough to hang,
While at my Lines the Fishes twang!

But now away my Hooks, my Quills,
And Angles, idle Utensils.
The *young Maria* walks to night:
Hide trifling Youth thy Pleasures slight.
'Twere shame that such judicious Eyes
Should with such Toyes a Man surprize;
She that already is the *Law*
Of all her *Sex*, her *Ages Aw.*

See how loose Nature, in respect
To her, it self doth recollect;
And every thing so whisht and fine,
Starts forthwith to its *Bonne Mine.*
The *Sun* himself, of *Her* aware,
Seems to descend with greater Care;
And lest *She* see him go to Bed,
In blushing Clouds conceales his Head.

So when the Shadows laid asleep
From underneath these Banks do creep,
And on the River as it flows
With *Eben Shuts* begin to close;
The modest *Halcyon* comes in sight,
Flying betwixt the Day and Night;
And such an horror calm and dumb,
Admiring Nature does benum.

The viscous Air, wheres'ere She fly,
Follows and sucks her Azure dy;
The gellying Stream compacts below,
If it might fix her shadow so;
The stupid Fishes hang, as plain
As *Flies* in *Chrystal* overt'ane;
And Men the silent *Scene* assist,
Charm'd with the *Saphir-winged Mist.*

Maria such, and so doth hush
The *World,* and through the *Ev'ning* rush.
No new-born *Comet* such a Train
Draws through the Skie, nor Star new-slain.
For streight those giddy Rockets fail,
Which from the putrid Earth exhale,
But by her *Flames,* in *Heaven* try'd,
Nature is wholly *vitrifi'd.*

'Tis *She* that to these Gardens gave
That wondrous Beauty which they have;
She streightness on the Woods bestows;
To *Her* the Meadow sweetness owes;
Nothing could make the River be
So Chrystal-pure but only *She*;
She yet more Pure, Sweet, Streight, and Fair,
Than Gardens, Woods, Meads, Rivers are.

Therefore what first *She* on them spent,
They gratefully again present.
The Meadow Carpets where to tread;
The Garden Flow'rs to Crown *Her* Head;
And for a Glass the limpid Brook,
Where *She* may all *her* Beautyes look;
But, since *She* would not have them seen,
The Wood about *her* draws a Skreen.

For *She*, to higher Beauties rais'd,
Disdains to be for lesser prais'd.
She counts her Beauty to converse
In all the Languages as hers;
Nor yet in those *her self* imployes
But for the *Wisdome*, not the *Noyse*;
Nor yet that *Wisdome* would affect,
But as 'tis *Heavens Dialect*.

Blest Nymph! that couldst so soon prevent
Those *Trains* by Youth against thee meant;
Tears (watry Shot that pierce the Mind;)
And *Sighs* (Loves Cannon charg'd with Wind;)
True Praise (That breaks through all defence;)
And *feign'd complying Innocence*;
But knowing where this *Ambush* lay,
She scap'd the safe, but roughest Way.

This 'tis to have been from the first
In a *Domestick Heaven* nurst;
Under the *Discipline* severe
Of *Fairfax*, and the starry *Vere*;
Where not one object can come nigh
But pure, and spotless as the Eye;
And *Goodness* doth it self intail
On *Females*, if there want a *Male*.

Go now fond Sex that on your Face
Do all your useless Study place,
Nor once at Vice your Brows dare knit
Lest the smooth Forehead wrinkled sit:
Yet your own Face shall at you grin,
Thorough the Black-bag of your Skin;
When *knowledge* only could have fill'd
And *Virtue* all of those *Furrows till'd*.

Hence *She* with Graces more divine
Supplies beyond her *Sex* the *Line*;
And, like a *sprig of Misleto*,
On the *Fairfacian Oak* does grow;
Whence, for some universal good,
The *Priest* shall cut the sacred Bud;
While her *glad Parents* most rejoice,
And make their *Destiny* their *Choice*.

Mean time ye Fields, Springs, Bushes, Flow'rs,
Where yet She leads her studious Hours,
(Till Fate her worthily translates,
And find a *Fairfax* for our *Thwaites*)
Employ the means you have by Her,
And in your kind your selves preferr;
That, as all *Virgins* She precedes,
So you all *Woods, Streams, Gardens, Meads.*

For you *Thessalian Tempe's Seat*
Shall now be scorn'd as obsolete;
Aranjuez, as less, disdain'd;
The *Bel-Retiro* as constrain'd;
But name not the *Idalian Grove*,
For 'twas the seat of wanton Love;
Much less the Deads' *Elysian Feilds*,
Yet nor to them your Beauty yeilds.

'Tis not, what once it was, the *World*;
But a rude heap together hurl'd;
All negligently overthrown,
Gulfes, Deserts, Precipices, Stone.
Your lesser World contains the same.
But in more decent Order tame;
You Heaven's Center, Nature's Lap.
And Paradice's only Map.

But now the *Salmon-Fishers* moist
Their *Leathern Boats* begin to hoist;
And, like *Antipodes* in Shoes,
Have shod theyr *Heads* in their *Canoos.*
How Tortoise like, but not so slow,
These rational *Amphibii* go?
Let's in: for the dark *Hemisphere*
Does now like one of them appear.

EPIGRAM ON THE TWO MOUNTAINS
OF *AMOS-CLIFF* AND *BILBOROUGH*
To *Fairfax*

Behold how Almias-cliff and Bilborough's brow
Mark with huge bounds the spacious plain below!
Dauntless, on that, the rocky turrets frown,
This the tall ash adorns with cheerful crown;
There the rough rocks in terrors grim are dress'd,
Here the smooth hill displays a verdant crest;
That height, like *Atlas*, seems to prop the skies,
But this beneath *Herculean* shoulders lies;
This, as a cell or grove, contracts the gaze,
That, as a goal, his head from far displays;
There *Pelion* on *Ossa* heaves amain,
Here some sweet nymph of *Pindus* leads her train.
The steep, the rough, the difficult, are there;
Here all is sloping, gentle, soft and fair.
But Nature doth both characters display
In *Fairfax*, whom with awe they both obey,
And, as his car rolls by, alike do feel
The impartial touch of his triumphant wheel.
Stern to the foe, and mild to him that yields,
His habits drawn from his paternal fields;
Here, with a woody strait between, one sees
The Pillars (in the North) of *Hercules*;
Or rather, since their bow'd tops thus agree,
Let them, *Maria*, thy *Parnassus* be!

OF POETRY AND
MUSIC

ON MR. *MILTON'S* PARADISE LOST

When I behold the Poet blind, yet bold,
In slender Book his vast Design unfold,
Messiah Crown'd, *Gods* Reconcil'd Decree,
Rebelling *Angels*, the Forbidden Tree,
Heav'n, Hell, Earth, Chaos, All; the Argument
Held me a while, misdoubting his Intent,
That he would ruine (for I saw him strong)
The sacred Truths to Fable and old Song,
(So *Sampson* groap'd the Temples Posts in spight)
The World o'rewhelming to revenge his Sight.

Yet as I read, soon growing less severe,
I lik'd his Project, the success did fear;
Through that wide Field how he his way should find
O're which lame Faith leads Understanding blind;
Lest he perplext the things he would explain,
And what was easie he should render vain.

Or if a Work so infinite he spann'd,
Jealous I was that some less skilful hand
(Such as disquiet alwayes what is well,
And by ill imitating would excell)
Might hence presume the whole Creations day
To change in Scenes, and show it in a Play.

Pardon me, *mighty Poet*, nor despise
My causeless, yet not impious, surmise.
But I am now convinc'd and none will dare
Within thy Labours to pretend a Share.

139

Thou hast not miss'd one thought that could be fit,
And all that was improper dost omit:
So that no room is here for Writers left,
But to detect their Ignorance or Theft.

That Majesty which through thy Work doth Reign
Draws the Devout, deterring the Profane.
And things divine thou treatst of in such state
As them preserves, and Thee, inviolate.
At once delight and horrour on us seize,
Thou singst with so much gravity and ease;
And above humane flight dost soar aloft,
With Plume so strong, so equal, and so soft.
The *Bird* nam'd from that *Paradise* you sing
So never Flags, but alwaies keeps on Wing.

Where couldst thou Words of such a compass find?
Whence furnish such a vast expense of Mind?
Just Heav'n Thee, like *Tiresias*, to requite,
Rewards with *Prophesie* thy loss of Sight.

Well might thou scorn thy Readers to allure
With tinkling Rhime, of thy own Sense secure;
While the *Town-Bays* writes all the while and spells,
And like a Pack-Horse tires without his Bells.
Their Fancies like our bushy Points appear,
The Poets tag them; we for fashion wear.
I, too, transported by the *Mode* offend,
And while I meant to *Praise* thee, must Commend.
Thy verse created like thy *Theme* sublime,
In Number, Weight, and Measure, needs not *Rhime*.

TO HIS NOBLE FRIEND MR. *RICHARD LOVELACE*, UPON HIS POEMS

   Sir,
Our times are much degenerate from those
Which your sweet Muse, which your fair Fortune chose,
And as complexions alter with the Climes,
Our wits have drawne th' infections of our times.
That candid Age no other way could tell
To be ingenious, but by speaking well.
Who best could prayse, had then the greatest prayse,
'Twas more esteemed to give, than weare the Bayes:
Modest ambition studi'd only then,
To honor not her selfe, but worthy men.
These vertues now are banisht out of Towne,
Our Civill Wars have lost the Civicke crowne.
He highest builds, who with most Art destroys,
And against others Fame his owne employs.
I see the envious Caterpillar sit
On the faire blossome of each growing wit.
   The Ayre's already tainted with the swarms
Of Insects which against you rise in arms.
Word-peckers, Paper-rats, Book-scorpions,
Of wit corrupted, the unfashion'd Sons.
The barbed Censurers begin to looke
Like the grim consistory on thy Booke:
And on each line cast a reforming eye,

Severer than the yong Presbytery.
Till when in vaine they have thee all perus'd,
You shall for being faultless be accus'd.
Some reading your *Lucasta*, will alledge
You wrong'd in her the Houses Priviledge.
Some that you under sequestration are,
Because you write when going to the Warre,
And one the book prohibits, because *Kent*
Their first Petition by the Authour sent.

    But when the beauteous Ladies came to know
That their deare *Lovelace* was endanger'd so:
Lovelace that thaw'd the most congealed brest,
He who lov'd best and them defended best.
Whose hand so rudely grasps the steely brand,
Whose hand so gently melts the Ladies hand.
They all in mutiny though yet undrest
Sally'd, and would in his defence contest.
And one the loveliest that was yet e're seen,
Thinking that I too of the rout had been.
Mine eyes invaded with a female spight,
(She knew what pain 'twould be to lose that sight.)
O no, mistake not, I reply'd, for I
In your defence, or in his cause would dy.
But he secure of glory and of time
Above their envy or mine aid doth clime.
Him, valiant men, and fairest Nymphs approve,
His Booke in them finds Judgement, with you Love.

TO HIS WORTHY FRIEND DOCTOR
WITTY UPON HIS TRANSLATION OF
THE POPULAR ERRORS

Sit further, and make room for thine own fame,
Where just desert enrolles thy honour'd Name
The good Interpreter. Some in this task
Take off the Cypress vail, but leave a mask,
Changing the Latine, but do more obscure
That sence in *English*, which was bright and pure.
So of Translators they are Authors grown,
For ill Translators make the Book their own.
Others do strive with words and forced phrase
To add such lustre, and so many rayes,
That but to make the Vessel shining, they
Much of the precious Metal rub away.
He is Translation's thief that addeth more,
As much as he that taketh from the Store
Of the First Author. Here he maketh blots
That mends; and added beauties are but spots.
   Celia whose English doth more richly flow
Than *Tagus*, purer than dissolved snow.
And sweet as are her lips that speak it, she
Now learns the tongues of *France* and *Italy*;
But she is *Celia* still: no other grace
But her own smiles commend that lovely face;
Her native beauty's not Italianated,

Nor her chaste mind into the *French* translated:
Her thoughts are *English*, though her sparkling wit
With other Language doth them fitly fit.
    Translators learn of her: but stay, I slide
Down into Error with the Vulgar tide;
Women must not teach here: the Doctor doth
Stint them to Cawdles, Almond-milk, and Broth.
Now I reform, and surely so will all
Whose happy Eyes on thy Translation fall,
I see the people hastning to thy Book,
Liking themselves the worse the more they look,
And so disliking, that they nothing see
Now worth the liking, but thy Book and thee.
And (if I Judgment have) I censure right;
For something guides, my hand that I must write.
You have Translations statutes best fulfil'd.
That handling neither sully nor would guild.

UPON AN EUNUCH; A POET
(Fragment)

Nec sterilem te crede; licet, mulieribus exul,
Falcem virginiae nequeas immittere messi,
Et nostro peccare modo. Tibi Fama perennè
Proegnabit; rapiesque novem de monte Sorores;
Et pariet modulos *Echo* repetita Nepotes.

TRANSLATION

Deem not that thou art barren, though, forlorn,
Thou plunge no sickle in the virgin corn,
And, mateless, hast no part in our sweet curse.
Fame shall be ever pregnant by thy verse;
The vocal Sisters nine thou shalt embrace,
And *Echo* nurse thy words, a tuneful race.

MUSICKS EMPIRE

First was the World as one great Cymbal made,
Where Jarring Windes to infant Nature plaid.
All Musick was a solitary sound,
To hollow Rocks and murm'ring Fountains bound.

Jubal first made the wilder Notes agree;
And *Jubal* tun'd Musick's first *Jubilee*:
He call'd the *Ecchoes* from their sullen Cell,
And built the Organs City where they dwell.

Each sought a consort in that lovely place;
And Virgin Trebles wed the manly Base.
From whence the Progeny of numbers new
Into harmonious Colonies withdrew.

Some to the Lute, some to the Viol went,
And others chose the Cornet eloquent.
These practising the Wind, and those the Wire,
To sing Mens Triumphs, or in Heavens quire.

Then Musick, the Mosaique of the Air,
Did of all these a solemn noise prepare:
With which She gain'd the Empire of the Ear,
Including all between the Earth and Sphear.

Victorious sounds! yet here your Homage do
Unto a gentler Conqueror than you;
Who though He flies the Musick of his praise,
Would with you Heavens Hallelujahs raise.

FLECKNO, AN ENGLISH PRIEST AT *ROME*

Oblig'd by frequent visits of this man,
Whom as Priest, Poet, and Musician,
I for some branch of *Melchizedeck* took,
(Though he derives himself from *my Lord Brooke*)
I sought his Lodging; which is at the Sign
Of the sad *Pelican*; Subject divine
For Poetry: There three Stair-Cases high,
Which signifies his triple property,
I found at last a Chamber, as 'twas said,
But seem'd a Coffin set on the Stairs head,
Not higher than Seav'n, nor larger than three feet;
Only there was nor Seeling, nor a Sheet,
Save that th' ingenious Door did as you come
Turn in, and shew to Wainscot half the Room.
Yet of his State no man could have complain'd;
There being no Bed where he entertain'd:
And though within one Cell so narrow pent,
He'd *Stanzas* for a whole Appartement.
    Straight, without further information,
In hideous verse, he, and a dismal tone,
Begins to exorcise, as if I were
Possest, and sure the *Devil* brought me there.
But I, who now imagin'd my self brought
To my last Tryal, in a serious thought
Calm'd the disorders of my youthful Breast,

And to my Martyrdom prepared Rest.
Only this frail Ambition did remain,
The last distemper of the sober Brain,
That there had been some present to assure
The future Ages how I did indure:
And how I, silent, turn'd my burning Ear
Towards the Verse: and when that could not hear,
Held him the other; and unchanged yet,
Ask'd still for more, and pray'd him to repeat:
Till the Tyrant, weary to persecute,
Left off, and try'd t' allure me with his Lute.
   Now as two Instruments, to the same key
Being tun'd by Art, if the one touched be
The other opposite as soon replies,
Mov'd by the Air and hidden Sympathies;
So while he with his gouty Fingers craules
Over the Lute, his murmuring Belly calls,
Whose hungry Guts to the same streightness twin'd
In Echo to the trembling Strings repin'd.
   I, that perceiv'd now what his Musick ment,
Ask'd civilly if he had eat this Lent.
He answered yes, with such, and such an one;
For he has this of gen'rous, that alone
He never feeds, save only when he tryes
With gristly Tongue to dart the passing Flyes.

I ask'd if he eat flesh. And he, that was
So hungry that though ready to say *Mass*
Would break his fast before, said he was Sick,
And th' *Ordinance* was only Politick.
Nor was I longer to invite him: Scant
Happy at once to make him Protestant,
And Silent. Nothing now Dinner stay'd
But till he had himself a Body made.
I mean till he were drest: for else so thin
He stands, as if he only fed had been
With consecrated Wafers: and the *Host*
Hath sure more flesh and blood than he can boast.
This *Basso Relievo* of a Man,
Who as a Camel tall, yet easily can
The Needle's Eye thread without any stich,
(His only impossible is to be rich)
Lest his too suttle Body, growing rare,
Should leave his Soul to wander in the Air,
He therefore circumscribes himself in rimes;
And swaddled in's own papers seaven times,
Wears a close Jacket of poetick Buff,
With which he doth his third Dimension Stuff.
Thus armed underneath, he over all
Does make a primitive *Sotana* fall;
And above that yet casts an antick Cloak,
Worn at the first Counsel of *Antioch*;
Which by the *Jews* long hid, and Disesteem'd,

He heard of by Tradition, and redeem'd.
But were he not in this black habit deck't,
This half transparent Man would soon reflect
Each colour that he past by; and be seen,
As the *Chamelion*, yellow, blew, or green.
    He drest, and ready to disfurnish now
His Chamber, whose compactness did allow
No empty place for complimenting doubt,
But who came last is forc'd first to go out;
I meet one on the Stairs who made me stand,
Stopping the passage, and did him demand:
I answer'd he is here *Sir*; but you see
You cannot pass to him but thorow me.
He thought himself affronted; and reply'd,
I whom the Pallace never has deny'd
Wil make the way here; I said *Sir* you'l do
Me a great favour, for I seek to go.
He gath'ring fury still made sign to draw;
But himself there clos'd in a Scabbard saw
As narrow as his Sword's; and I, that was
Delightful, said there can no Body pass
Except by penetration hither, where
Two make a crowd, nor can three Persons here
Consist but in one substance. Then, to fit
Our peace, the Priest said I too had some wit:
To prov't, I said, the place doth us invite
By its own narrowness, Sir, to unite.

He ask'd me pardon; and to make me way
Went down, as I him follow'd to obey.
But the propitiatory Priest had straight
Oblig'd us, when below, to celebrate
Together our attonement: so increas'd
Betwixt us two the Dinner to a Feast.

Let it suffice that we could eat in peace;
And that both Poems did and Quarrels cease
During the Table; though my new made Friend
Did, as he threatned, ere 'twere long, intend
To be both witty and valiant: I loth,
Said 'twas too late, he was already both.

But now, Alas, my first Tormentor came,
Who satisfy'd with eating, but not tame,
Turns to recite; though Judges most severe
After th' Assizes dinner mild appear,
And on full stomach do condemn but few:
Yet he more strict my sentence doth renew,
And draws out of the black box of his Breast
Ten quire of paper in which he was drest.
Yet that which was a greater cruelty
Than *Nero's* Poem he calls charity,
And so the *Pelican* at his door hung
Picks out the tender bosome to its young.

Of all his Poems there he stands ungirt
Save only two foul copies for his shirt:
Yet these he promises as soon as clean.

But how I loath'd to see my Neighbour glean
Those papers, which he pilled from within
Like white fleaks rising from a Leper's skin!
More odious than those raggs which the *French* youth
At ordinaries after dinner show'th,
When they compare their *Chancres* and *Poulains.*
Yet he first kist them, and after takes pains
To read; and then, because he understood
Not one Word, thought and swore that they were good.
But all his praises could not now appease
The provok't Author, whom it did displease
To hear his Verses, by so just a curse,
That were ill made, condemn'd to be read worse:
And how (impossible) he made yet more
Absurdityes in them than were before.
For he his untun'd voice did fall or raise
As a deaf Man upon a Viol playes,
Making the half points and the periods run
Confus'der than the atoms in the Sun.
Thereat the Poet swell'd, with anger full,
And roar'd out, like *Perillus* in's own *Bull*;
Sir you read false. That any one but you
Should know the contrary. Whereat, I, now
Made Mediator, in my room, said, Why?
To say that you read false *Sir* is no Lye.
Thereat the waxen Youth relented straight;
But saw with sad dispair that 'twas too late.

For the disdainful Poet was retir'd
Home, his most furious Satyr to have fir'd
Against the Rebel; who, at this struck dead,
Wept bitterly as disinherited.
Who should commend his Mistress now? Or who
Praise him? both difficult indeed to do
With truth. I counsell'd him to go in time,
Ere the fierce Poet's anger turn'd to rime.
    He hasted; and I, finding my self free,
As one scap't strangely from Captivity,
Have made the Chance be painted; and go now
To hang it in *Saint Peter's* for a Vow.

OF PUBLIC AFFAIRS

AN *HORATIAN* ODE UPON *CROMWEL'S* RETURN FROM *IRELAND*

The forward Youth that would appear
Must now forsake his *Muses* dear,
    Nor in the Shadows sing
    His Numbers languishing.
'Tis time to leave the Books in dust,
And oyl th' unused Armours rust:
    Removing from the Wall
    The Corslet of the Hall.
So restless *Cromwel* could not cease
In the inglorious Arts of Peace,
    But through adventrous War
    Urged his active Star:
And, like the three-fork'd Lightning, first
Breaking the Clouds where it was nurst,
    Did thorough his own Side
    His fiery way divide.
For 'tis all one to Courage high
The Emulous or Enemy;
    And with such to inclose
    Is more then to oppose.
Then burning through the Air he went,
And Pallaces and Temples rent:

And *Cæsars* head at last
 Did through his Laurels blast.
'Tis Madness to resist or blame
The force of angry Heavens flame;
 And, if we would speak true,
 Much to the Man is due:
Who, from his private Gardens, where
He liv'd reserved and austere,
 As if his highest plot
 To plant the Bergamot,
Could by industrious Valour climbe
To ruine the great Work of Time,
 And cast the Kingdoms old
 Into another Mold.
Though Justice against Fate complain,
And plead the antient Rights in vain:
 But those do hold or break
 As Men are strong or weak.
Nature that hateth emptiness,
Allows of penetration less:
 And therefore must make room
 Where greater Spirits come.
What Field of all the Civil Wars
Where his were not the deepest Scars?
 And *Hampton* shows what part
 He had of wiser Art:
Where, twining subtile fears with hope,

He wove a Net of such a scope,
  That *Charles* himself might chase
  To *Caresbrooks* narrow case:
That thence the *Royal Actor* born
The *Tragick Scaffold* might adorn,
  While round the armed Bands
  Did clap their bloody hands.
He nothing common did, or mean,
Upon the memorable Scene:
  But with his keener Eye
  The Axes edge did try:
Nor call'd the *Gods* with vulgar spight
To vindicate his helpless Right,
  But bow'd his comely Head
  Down, as upon a Bed.
This was that memorable Hour
Which first assur'd the forced Pow'r.
  So when they did design
  The *Capitols* first Line,
A bleeding Head where they begun,
Did fright the Architects to run;
  And yet in that the *State*
  Foresaw its happy Fate.
And now the *Irish* are asham'd
To see themselves in one Year tam'd:
  So much one Man can do,
  That does both act and know.

They can affirm his Praises best,
And have, though overcome, confest
    How good he is, how just,
    And fit for highest Trust:
Nor yet grown stiffer with Command,
But still in the *Republick's* hand:
    How fit he is to sway
    That can so well obey.
He to the *Commons Feet* presents
A *Kingdome*, for his first years rents:
    And, what he may, forbears
    His Fame to make it theirs:
And has his Sword and Spoyls ungirt,
To lay them at the *Publick's* skirt.
    So when the Falcon high
    Falls heavy from the Sky,
She, having kill'd, no more does search,
But on the next green Bow to pearch;
    Where, when he first does lure,
    The Falckner has her sure.
What may not then our *Isle* presume
While Victory his Crest does plume;
    What may not others fear,
    If thus he crown each Year!
A *Cæsar* he ere long to *Gaul*,
To *Italy* an *Hannibal*,
    And to all States not free

Shall *Clymacterick* be.
The *Pict* no shelter now shall find
Within his party-colour'd Mind;
  But from this Valour sad
  Shrink underneath the Plad:
Happy if in the tufted brake
The *English Hunter* him mistake,
  Nor lay his Hounds in near
  The *Caledonian* Deer.
But thou the Wars and Fortunes Son
March indefatigably on,
  And for the last effect
  Still keep thy Sword erect:
Besides the force it has to fright
The Spirits of the shady Night;
  The same *Arts* that did *gain*
  A *Pow'r* must it *maintain*.

THE CHARACTER OF *HOLLAND*

Holland, that scarce deserves the name of *Land*,
As but th' Off-scouring of the *Brittish Sand*;
And so much Earth as was contributed
By *English Pilots* when they heav'd the Lead;
Or what by th' Oceans slow alluvion fell,
Of shipwrackt Cockle and the Muscle-shell;
This indigested vomit of the Sea
Fell to the *Dutch* by just Propriety.

Glad then, as Miners that have found the Ore,
They with mad labour fish'd the *Land* to *Shoar*;
And div'd as desperately for each piece
Of Earth, as if't had been of *Ambergreece*;
Collecting anxiously small Loads of Clay,
Less than what building Swallows bear away;
Or than those Pills which sordid Beetles roul,
Transfusing into them their Dunghil Soul.

How did they rivet, with Gigantick Piles,
Thorough the Center their new-catched Miles;
And to the stake a strugling Country bound,
Where barking Waves still bait the forced Ground;
Building their *watry Babel* far more high
To reach the *Sea*, than those to scale the *Sky*?

Yet still his claim the injur'd Ocean laid,
And oft at Leap-frog ore their Steeples plaid:
As if on purpose it on Land had come

To shew them what's their *Mare Liberum*.
A daily deluge over them does boyl;
The Earth and Water play at *Level-coyl*;
The Fish oft-times the Burger dispossest,
And sat not as a Meat but as a Guest;
And oft the *Tritons* and the *Sea-Nymphs* saw
Whole sholes of *Dutch* serv'd up for *Cabillau*;
Or as they over the new Level rang'd
For pickled *Herring*, pickled *Heeren* chang'd.
Nature, it seem'd, asham'd of her mistake,
Would throw their Land away at *Duck* and *Drake*.

    Therefore *Necessity*, that first made *Kings*,
Something like *Government* among them brings.
For as with *Pygmees* who best kills the *Crane*,
Among the *hungry* he that treasures *Grain*,
Among the *blind* the one-ey'd *blinkard* reigns,
So rules among the *drowned* he that *draines*.
Not who first sees the *rising Sun* commands,
But who could first discern the *rising Lands*.
Who best could know to pump an Earth so leak,
Him they their *Lord* and *Country's Father* speak.
To make a *Bank* was a great *Plot of State*;
Invent a *Shov'l* and be a *Magistrate*.
Hence some small *Dyke-grave* unperceiv'd invades
The *Pow'r*, and grows as 'twere a *King of Spades*.
But for less envy some *joynt States* endures,
Who look like a *Commission of the Sewers*.

For these *Half-anders*, half wet, and half dry,
Nor bear *strict service*, nor *pure Liberty*.
  'Tis probable *Religion* after this
Came next in order; which they could not miss,
How could the *Dutch* but be converted, when
Th' *Apostles* were so many Fishermen?
Besides the Waters of themselves did rise,
And, as their Land, so them did re-baptize.
Though *Herring* for their *God* few voices mist,
And *Poor-John* to have been th' *Evangelist*.
Faith, that could never Twins conceive before,
Never so fertile, spawn'd upon this shore:
More pregnant then their *Marg'ret*, that laid down
For *Hans-in-Kelder* of a whole *Hans-Town*.
  Sure when *Religion* did it self imbark,
And from the *East* would *Westward* steer its Ark,
It struck, and splitting on this unknown ground,
Each one thence pillag'd the first piece he found;
Hence *Amsterdam*, *Turk-Christian-Pagan-Jew*,
Staple of Sects and Mint of Schisme grew;
That *Bank of Conscience*, where not one so strange
Opinion but finds Credit, and Exchange.
In vain for *Catholicks* our selves we bear;
The *universal Church* is onely there.
Nor can Civility there want for *Tillage*,
Where wisely for their *Court* they chose a *Village*.
How fit a Title clothes their *Governours*,

Themselves the *Hogs* as all their Subjects *Bores*!
   Let it suffice to give their Country Fame
That it had one *Civilis* call'd by Name,
Some Fifteen hundred and more years ago;
But surely never any that was so.
   See but their *Mairmaids* with their *Tails of Fish*,
Reeking at *Church* over the *Chafing-Dish*.
A vestal Turf enshrin'd in Earthen Ware
Fumes through the loop-holes of a wooden Square.
Each to the *Temple* with these *Altars* tend,
But still does place it at her *Western End*:
While the fat steam of *Female Sacrifice*
Fills the *Priests Nostrils* and puts out his *Eyes*.
   Or what a Spectacle the *Skipper gross*,
A water-Hercules Butter-Coloss,
Tunn'd up with all their sev'ral *Towns of Beer*;
When Stagg'ring upon some Land, *Snick and Sneer*,
They try, like Statuaries, if they can
Cut out each others *Athos* to a Man:
And carve in their large Bodies, where they please,
The Armes of the *United Provinces*.
   But when such Amity at home is show'd;
What then are their confederacies abroad?
Let this one court'sie witness all the rest;
When their whole Navy they together prest,
Not Christian Captives to redeem from Bands:
Or intercept the Western golden Sands:

No, but all ancient Rights and Leagues must vail,
Rather than to the *English* strike their sail;
To whom their weather beaten *Province* ows
It self, when at some greater Vessel tows
A Cock-boat tost with the same wind and fate,
We buoy'd so often up their *sinking State*.
   Was this *Jus Belli & Pacis*; could this be
Cause why their *Burgomaster of the Sea*
Ram'd with Gun-powder, flaming with Brand wine,
Should raging hold his Linstock to the Mine?
While, with feign'd *Treaties*, they invade by stealth
Our sore new circumcised *Common wealth*.
   Yet of his vain Attempt no more he sees
Then of *Case-Butter* shot and *Bullet-Cheese*.
And the torn Navy stagger'd with him home,
While the Sea laught it self into a foam,
'Tis true since that (as fortune kindly sports,)
A wholesome Danger drove us to our Ports.
While half their banish'd keels the Tempest tost,
Half bound at home in Prison to the frost:
That ours mean time at leizure might careen,
In a calm Winter, under Skies Serene.
As the obsequious Air and Waters rest,
Till the dear *Halcyon* hatch out all its nest.
The *Common wealth* doth by its losses grow;
And, like its own Seas, only Ebbs to flow.
Besides that very Agitation laves,

And purges out the corruptible waves.
    And now again our armed *Bucentore*
Doth yearly their *Sea-Nuptials* restore.
And now the *Hydra of seaven Provinces*
Is strangled by our *Infant Hercules.*
Their Tortoise wants its vainly stretched neck;
Their Navy all our Conquest or our Wreck:
Or, what is left, their *Carthage* overcome
Would render fain unto our better *Rome,*
Unless our *Senate,* lest their Youth disuse
The War, (but who would) Peace if begg'd refuse.
    For now of nothing may our *State* despair,
Darling of Heaven, and of Men the Care;
Provided that they be what they have been,
Watchful abroad, and honest still within.
For while our *Neptune* doth a *Trident* shake,
Steel'd with those piercing Heads, *Dean, Monk,*
        and *Blake,*
And while *Jove* governs in the highest Sphere,
Vainly in *Hell* let *Pluto* domineer.

THE FIRST ANNIVERSARY OF THE GOVERNMENT UNDER HIS HIGHNESS THE LORD PROTECTOR

    Like the vain Curlings of the Watry maze,
Which in smooth Streams a sinking Weight dos raise;
So Man, declining always, disappears
In the weak Circles of increasing Years;
And his short Tumults of themselves Compose,
While flowing Time above his Head does close.
    Cromwell alone with greater Vigour runs,
(Sun-like) the Stages of succeeding Suns:
And still the Day which he doth next restore,
Is the just Wonder of the Day before.
Cromwell alone doth with new Lustre spring,
And shines the Jewell of the yearly Ring.
    'Tis he the force of scatter'd Time contracts,
And in one Year the work of Ages acts:
While heavie Monarchs make a wide Return,
Longer, and more Malignant then *Saturn*:
And though they all *Platonique* years should raign,
In the same Posture would be found again.
Their earthy Projects under ground they lay,
More slow and brittle then the *China* clay:
Well may they strive to leave them to their Son,
For one Thing never was by one King don.
Yet some more active for a Frontier Town

Took in by Proxie, beggs a false Renown;
Another triumphs at the publique Cost,
And will have Wonn, if he no more have Lost;
They fight by Others, but in Person wrong,
And only are against their Subjects strong;
Their other Wars seem but a feign'd contest,
This Common Enemy is still opprest;
If Conquerors, on them they turn their might;
If Conquered, on them they wreak their Spight:
They neither build the Temple in their dayes,
Nor Matter for succeeding Founders raise;
Nor sacred Prophecies consult within,
Much less themselves to perfect them begin;
No other care they bear of things above,
But with Astrologers divine, and *Jove*,
To know how long their Planet yet Reprives
From the deserved Fate their guilty lives:
Thus (Image-like) an useless time they tell,
And with vain Scepter strike the hourly Bell;
Nor more contribute to the state of Things,
Than wooden Heads unto the Violls strings.

    While indefatigable *Cromwell* hyes,
And cuts his way still nearer to the Skyes,

Learning a Musique in the Region clear,
To tune this lower to that higher Sphere.

    So when *Amphion* did the Lute command,
Which the God gave him, with his gentle hand,
The rougher Stones, unto his Measures hew'd,
Dans'd up in order from the Quarreys rude:
This took a Lower, that an Higher place,
As he the Treble alter'd, or the Base:
No Note he struck, but a new Story lay'd,
And the great Work ascended while he play'd.

    The listning Structures he with Wonder ey'd,
And still new Stopps to various Time apply'd:
Now through the Strings a Martial rage he throws,
And joyning streight the *Theban* Tow'r arose;
Then as he strokes them with a touch more sweet,
The flocking Marbles in a Palace meet;
But, for he most the graver Notes did try,
Therefore the Temples rear'd their Columns high:
Thus, ere he ceas'd, his sacred Lute creates
Th' harmonious City of the seven Gates.

    Such was that wondrous Order and Consent,
When *Cromwell* tun'd the ruling Instrument;
While tedious Statesmen many years did hack,
Framing a Liberty that still went back;
Whose num'rous Gorge could swallow in an hour
That Island, which the Sea cannot devour:
Then our *Amphion* issues out and sings,

170

And once he struck, and twice, the pow'rful Strings.

    The Commonwealth then first together came,
And each one enter'd in the willing Frame;
All other Matter yields, and may be rul'd;
But who the Minds of stubborn Men can build?
No Quarry bears a Stone so hardly wrought,
Nor with such labour from its Center brought:
None to be sunk in the Foundation bends,
Each in the House the highest Place contends,
And each the Hand that lays him will direct,
And some fall back upon the Architect;
Yet all compos'd by his attractive Song,
Into the Animated City throng.

    The Common-wealth does through their Centers all
Draw the Circumf'rence of the publique Wall;
The crossest Spirits here do take their part,
Fast'ning the Contignation which they thwart;
And they, whose Nature leads them to divide,
Uphold, this one, and that the other Side:
But the most Equall still sustein the Height,
And they as Pillars keep the Work upright;
While the resistance of opposed Minds,
The Fabrique as with Arches stronger binds,
Which on the Basis of a Senate free,
Knit by the Roofs Protecting weight agree.

    When for his Foot he thus a place had found,
He hurles e'r since the World about him round;

And in his sev'rall Aspects, like a Star,
Here shines in Peace, and thither shoots a War.
While by his Beams observing Princes steer,
And wisely court the Influence they fear;
O would they rather by his Pattern wonn,
Kiss the approaching, nor yet angry Sonn;
And in their numbred Footsteps humbly tread
The path where holy Oracles do lead;
How might they under such a Captain raise
The great Designes kept for the latter Dayes!
But mad with Reason, so miscall'd, of State
They know them not, and what they know not hate.
Hence still they sing Hosanna to the Whore,
And her whom they should Massacre adore:
But Indians whom they should convert, subdue;
Nor teach, but traffique with, or burn the Jew.

    Unhappy Princes, ignorantly bred,
By Malice some, by Errour more misled;
If gracious Heaven to my Life give length,
Leisure to Time, and to my Weakness Strength,
Then shall I once with graver Accents shake
Your Regall sloth, and your long Slumbers wake:
Like the shrill Huntsman that prevents the East,
Winding his Horn to Kings that chase the Beast.

    Till then my Muse shall hollow farr behind
Angelique *Cromwell* who outwings the wind;
And in dark Nights, and in cold Dayes alone

Pursues the Monster thorough every Throne:
Which shrinking to her *Roman* Denn impure,
Gnashes her Goary teeth; nor there secure.

   Hence oft I think, if in some happy Hour
High Grace should meet in one with highest Pow'r,
And then a seasonable People still
Should bend to his, as he to Heavens will,
What we might hope, what wonderfull Effect
From such a wish'd Conjuncture might reflect.
Sure, the mysterious Work, where none withstand,
Would forthwith finish under such a Hand:
Fore-shortned Time its useless Course would stay,
And soon precipitate the latest Day.
But a thick Cloud about that Morning lyes,
And intercepts the Beams of Mortall eyes,
That 'tis the most which we determine can,
If these the Times, then this must be the Man.
And well he therefore does, and well has guest,
Who in his Age has always forward prest:
And knowing not where Heavens choice may light,
Girds yet his Sword, and ready stands to fight;
But Men alass, as if they nothing car'd,
Look on, all unconcern'd, or unprepar'd;
And Stars still fall, and still the Dragons Tail
Swindges the Volumes of its horrid Flail.
For the great Justice that did first suspend
The World by Sinn, does by the same extend.

Hence that blest Day still counterpoysed wastes,
The Ill delaying, what th' Elected hastes;
Hence landing Nature to new Seas is tost,
And good Designes still with their Authors lost.

   And thou, great *Cromwell*, for whose happy birth
A Mold was chosen out of better Earth;
Whose Saint-like Mother we did lately see
Live out an Age, long as a Pedigree;
That shee might seem, could we the Fall dispute,
T'have smelt the Blossome, and not eat the Fruit;
Though none does of more lasting Parents grow,
But never any did them honor so;
Though thou thine Heart from Evil still unstain'd,
And always hast thy Tongue from fraud refrain'd;
Thou, who so oft through Storms of thundring Lead
Hast born securely thine undaunted Head,
Thy Brest though ponyarding Conspiracies,
Drawn from the Sheath of lying Prophecies;
Thee proof beyond all other Force or Skill,
Our Sinns endanger, and shall one day kill.

   How near they fail'd, and in thy sudden Fall
At once assay'd to overturn us all.
Our brutish fury strugling to be Free,
Hurry'd thy Horses while they hurry'd thee.
When thou hadst almost quit thy Mortall cares,
And soyl'd in Dust thy Crown of silver Hairs.

   Let this one Sorrow interweave among

The other Glories of our yearly Song.
Like skilful Looms which through the costly thred
Of purling Ore, a shining wave do shed.
So shall the Tears we on past Grief employ,
Still as they trickle, glitter in our Joy.
So with more Modesty we may be True,
And speak as of the Dead the Praises due:
While impious Men deceiv'd with pleasure short,
On their own Hopes shall find the Fall retort.

   But the poor Beasts wanting their noble Guide,
What could they more? shrunk guiltily aside.
First winged Fear transports them far away,
And leaden Sorrow then their flight did stay.
See how they each his towring Crest abate,
And the green Grass, and their known Mangers hate,
Nor through wide Nostrils snuffe the wanton aire,
Nor their round Hoofs, or curled Manes compare;
With wandring Eyes, and restless Ears they stood
And with shrill Neighings ask'd him of the Wood.

   Thou *Cromwell* falling not a stupid Tree,
Or Rock so savage, but it mourn'd for thee:
And all about was heard a Panique groan,
As if that Natures self were overthrown.
It seem'd the Earth did from the Center tear;
It seem'd the Sun was faln out of the Sphere:
Justice obstructed lay, and Reason fool'd;
Courage disheartned, and Religion cool'd.

A dismall Silence through the Palace went,
And then loud Shreeks the vaulted Marbles rent.
Such as the dying Chorus sings by turns,
And to deaf Seas, and ruthless Tempest mourns,
When now they sink, and now the plundring Streams
Break up each Deck, and rip the Oaken seams.

But thee triumphant hence the firy Carr,
And firy Steeds had born out of the Warr,
From the low World, and thankless Men above,
Unto the Kingdom blest of Peace and Love:
We only mourn'd our selves, in thine Ascent,
Whom thou hadst left beneath with Mantle rent.

For all delight of Life thou then didst lose,
When to Command, thou didst thy self Depose;
Resigning up thy Privacy so dear,
To turn the headstrong Peoples Charioteer;
For to be *Cromwell* was a greater thing,
Than ought below, or yet above a King:
Therefore thou rather didst thy Self depress,
Yielding to Rule, because it made thee Less.

For neither didst thou from the first apply
Thy sober Spirit unto things too High,
But in thine own Fields exercisedst long,
An healthfull Mind within a Body strong;
Till at the Seventh time thou in the Skyes,
As a small Cloud, like a Mans hand didst rise;
Then did thick Mists and Winds the aire deform,

And down at last thou pour'dst the fertile Storm;
Which to the thirsty Land did plenty bring,
But, though forewarn'd, o'r-took and wet the King.

What since he did, an higher Force him push'd
Still from behind, and it before him rush'd,
Though undiscern'd among the tumult blind,
Who think those high Decrees by Man design'd.
'Twas Heav'n would not that his Pow'r should cease,
But walk still middle betwixt Warr and Peace;
Choosing each Stone, and poysing every weight,
Trying the Measures of the Bredth and Height;
Here pulling down, and there erecting New,
Founding a firm State by Proportions true.

When *Gideon* so did from the Warr retreat,
Yet by the Conquest of two Kings grown great,
He on the Peace extends a Warlike power,
And *Is'rel* silent saw him rase the Tow'r;
And how he Succoths Elders durst suppress,
With Thorns and Briars of the Wilderness.
No King might ever such a Force have don;
Yet would not he be Lord, nor yet his Son.

Thou with the same strength, and an Heart as plain,
Didst (like thine Olive) still refuse to Reign;
Though why should others all thy Labor spoil,
And Brambles be anointed with thine Oil,
Whose climbing Flame, without a timely stop,
Had quickly Levell'd every Cedar's top.

Therefore first growing to thy self a Law,
Th' ambitious Shrubs thou in just time didst aw.

So have I seen at Sea, when whirling Winds,
Hurry the Bark, but more the Seamens minds,
Who with mistaken Course salute the Sand,
And threat'ning Rocks misapprehend for Land;
While balefull *Tritons* to the shipwrack guide,
And Corposants along the Tacklings slide.
The Passengers all wearyed out before,
Giddy, and wishing for the fatall Shore;
Some lusty Mate, who with more carefull Ey
Counted the Hours, and ev'ry Star did spy,
The Helm does from the artless Steersman strain,
And doubles back unto the safer Main.
What though a while they grumble discontent,
Saving himself he does their loss prevent.

'Tis not a Freedome, that where All command;
Nor Tyrannie, where One does them withstand:
But who of both the Bounders knows to lay
Him as their Father must the State obey.

Thou, and thine House, like *Noahs* Eight did rest,
Left by the Warrs Flood on the Mountains crest:
And the large Vale lay subject to thy Will,
Which thou but as an Husbandman wouldst Till:
And only didst for others plant the Vine
Of Liberty, not drunken with its Wine.

That sober Liberty which men may have,

That they enjoy, but more they vainly crave:
And such as to their Parents Tents do press,
May shew their own, not see his Nakedness.

Yet such a *Chammish* issue still does rage,
The Shame and Plague both of the Land and Age,
Who watch'd thy halting, and thy Fall deride,
Rejoycing when thy Foot had slipt aside;
That their new King might the fifth Scepter shake,
And make the World, by his Example, Quake:
Whose frantique Army should they want for Men
Might muster Heresies, so one were ten.
What thy Misfortune, they the Spirit call,
And their Religion only is to Fall.
Oh *Mahomet*! now couldst thou rise again,
Thy Falling sicknes should have made thee Reign,
While *Feake* and *Simpson* would in many a Tome,
Have writ the Comments of thy sacred Foame:
For soon thou mightst have past among their Rant
Wer't but for thine unmoved Tulipant;
As thou must needs have own'd them of thy band
For Prophecies fit to be *Alcorand*.

Accursed Locusts, whom your King does spit
Out of the Center of th' unbottom'd Pit;
Wand'rers, Adult'rers, Lyers, *Munser's* rest,
Sorcerers, Atheists, Jesuites, Possest;
You who the Scriptures and the Laws deface
With the same liberty as Points and Lace;

Oh Race most hypocritically strict!
Bent to reduce us to the ancient Pict;
Well may you act the *Adam* and the *Eve*,
Ay, and the Serpent too that did deceive.

   But the great Captain, now the danger's ore,
Makes you for his sake Tremble one fit more;
And, to your spight, returning yet alive
Does with himself all that is good revive.

   So when first Man did through the Morning new
See the bright Sun his shining Race pursue,
All day he follow'd with unwearied sight,
Pleas'd with that other World of moving Light;
But thought him when he miss'd his setting beams,
Sunk in the Hills, or plung'd below the Streams.
While dismal blacks hung round the Universe,
And Stars (like Tapers) burn'd upon his Herse:
And Owls and Ravens with their screeching noyse
Did make the Fun'rals sadder by their Joyes.
His weeping Eys the dolefull Vigills keep,
Not knowing yet the Night was made for sleep:
Still to the West, where he him lost, he turn'd,
And with such accents, as Despairing, mourn'd:
Why did mine Eyes once see so bright a Ray;
Or why Day last no longer than a Day?
When streight the Sun behind him he descry'd,
Smiling serenely from the further side.

   So while our Star that gives us Light and Heat,

Seem'd now a long and gloomy Night to threat,
Up from the other World his Flame he darts,
And Princes, shining through their windows, starts;
Who their suspected Counsellors refuse,
And credulous Ambassadors accuse.

   "Is this," saith one, "the Nation that we read
Spent with both Wars, under a Captain dead?
Yet rigg a Navie while we dress us late;
And ere we Dine, rase and rebuild their State.
What Oaken Forrests, and what golden Mines!
What Mints of Men, what Union of Designes!
Unless their Ships, do, as their Fowle proceed
Of shedding Leaves, that with their Ocean breed.
Theirs are not Ships, but rather Arks of War,
And beaked Promontories sail'd from farr;
Of floting Islands a new hatched Nest;
A Fleet of Worlds, of other Worlds in quest;
An hideous shole of wood-Leviathans,
Arm'd with three Tire of brazen Hurricans;
That through the Center shoot their thundring side
And sink the Earth that does at Anchor ride.
What refuge to escape them can be found,
Whose watry Leaguers all the world surround?
Needs must we all their Tributaries be,
Whose Navies hold the Sluces of the Sea.
The Ocean is the Fountain of Command,
But that once took, we Captives are on Land.

And those that have the Waters for their share,
Can quickly leave us neither Earth nor Aire.
Yet if through these our Fears could find a pass;
Through double Oak, and lin'd with treble Brass;
That one Man still, although but nam'd, alarms
More than all Men, all Navies, and all Arms.
Him, all the Day, Him, in late Nights I dread,
And still his Sword seems hanging ore my head.
The Nation had been ours, but his one Soule
Moves the great Bulk, and animates the whole.
He Secrecy with Number hath inchas'd,
Courage with Age, Maturity with Haste:
The Valiants Terror, Riddle of the Wise;
And still his Fauchion all our Knots unties.
Where did he learn those Arts that cost us dear?
Where below Earth, or where above the Sphere?
He seems a King by long Succession born,
And yet the same to be a King does scorn.
Abroad a King he seems, and something more,
At Home a Subject on the equall Floor.
O could I once him with our Title see,
So should I hope yet he might Dye as wee.
But let them write his Praise that love him best,
It grieves me sore to have thus much confest."

    Pardon, great Prince, if thus their Fear or Spight
More than our Love and Duty do thee Right.
I yield, nor further will the Prize contend;

So that we both alike may miss our End:
While thou thy venerable Head dost raise
As far above their Malice as my Praise.
And as the *Angell* of our Commonweal,
Troubling the Waters, yearly mak'st them Heal.

A POEM UPON THE DEATH OF HIS LATE HIGHNESSE THE LORD PROTECTOR

That Providence which had so long the care
Of *Cromwell's* head, and numbred ev'ry haire,
Now in it self (the Glasse where all appears)
Had seen the period of his golden yeares:
And thenceforth only did attend to trace
What Death might least so faire a Life deface.

The people, which what most they fear esteem,
Death when more horrid, so more noble deem,
And blame the last *Act*, like Spectators vaine,
Unlesse the *Prince* whom they applaud be slaine;
Nor Fate indeed can well refuse that right
To those that liv'd in Warre, to dye in Fight.

But long his *Valour* none had left that could
Indanger him, or *Clemency* that would:
And he whom Nature all for Peace had made
But angry Heaven unto Warre had sway'd,
And so lesse usefull where he most desir'd,
For what he least affected was admir'd,
Deserved yet an End whose ev'ry part
Should speak the wondrous softnesse of his Heart.

To *Love and Griefe* the fatall writt was sign'd
(Those nobler weaknesses of humane Kinde,
From which those Powers that issu'd the Decree,
Although immortall, found they were not free),

That they, to whom his brest still open lyes,
In gentle Passions should his Death disguise:
And leave suceeding Ages cause to mourne,
As long as Griefe shall weep, or Love shall burne.
    Streight does a slow and languishing Disease
Eliza, Natures and his darling, seize:
Her when an Infant, taken with her Charms,
He oft would flourish in his mighty Arms;
And, lest their force the tender burthen wrong,
Slacken the vigour of his Muscles strong;
Then to the Mother's brest her softly move,
Which, while she drain'd of Milke, she fill'd with Love:
But as with riper Years her Vertue grew,
And every minute adds a Lustre new;
When with Meridian height her Beauty shin'd,
And thorough that sparkled her fairer Mind;
When shee with Smiles serene in Words discreet
His hidden Soule at every turne could meet;
Then might y' ha' daily his Affection spy'd,
Doubling that knott which Destiny had ty'd;
While they by sense, not knowing, comprehend
How on each other both theyr Fates depend.
With her each day the pleasing Houres he shares,
And at her Aspect calmes his growing Cares:

Or with a Grand Sire's joy her children sees
Hanging about her neck or at his knees,
Hold fast, dear Infants, hold them both or none!
This will not stay when once the other's gone.

A silent fire now wastes those Limbs of Wax
And him within his tortur'd Image racks.
So the Flow'r with'ring which the Garden crown'd,
The sad Roote pines in secret under ground.
Each Groane he doubled and each Sigh he sigh'd
Repeated over to the restlesse Night;
No trembling String compos'd to numbers new
Answers the touch in Notes more sad, more true.
She, lest he grieve, hides what she can her pains,
And he to lessen hers his Sorrow feigns;
Yet both perceiv'd, yet both conceal'd their Skills,
And so diminishing increas'd their ills,
That whether by each other's Griefe they fell,
Or on their own redoubled, none can tell.

And now *Eliza's* purple Locks were shorn,
Where she so long her *Father's* Fate had worn,
And frequent Lightning to her Soule that flyes
Devides the Aire and opens all the Skyes:
And now his Life, suspended by her breath,
Ran out impetuously to hasting Death.
Like polish'd Mirrours so his steely Brest
Had every figure of her woes exprest,
And with the damp of her last Gasps obscur'd

Had drawn such staines as were not to be cur'd.
Fate could not either reach with single stroke,
But, the dear Image fled, the Mirrour broke.

Who now shall tell us more of mournfull Swans,
Of Halcyons kinde, or bleeding Pelicans?
No downy brest did ere so gently beate,
Or fanne with airy plumes so soft an heat.
For he no duty by his height excus'd,
Nor, though a *Prince*, to be a *Man* refus'd;
But rather than in his *Eliza's* paine
Not love, not grieve, would neither live nor reigne;
And in himself so oft immortall try'd,
Yet in compassion of another dy'd.

So have I seen a Vine whose lasting Age
Of many a Winter hath surviv'd the rage,
Under whose shady tent Men every yeare
At its rich blood's expence their Sorrows cheare,
If some deare branch where it extends its life
Chance to be prun'd by an untimely Knife,
The Parent tree unto the Griefe succeeds,
And through the Wound its vital humour bleeds;
Trickling in watry drops, whose flowing shape
Weeps that it falls ere fix'd into a Grape.
So the dry Stock, no more that spreading Vine,
Frustrates the Autumne and the hopes of Wine.

A secret Cause does sure those Signes ordaine
Foreboding Princes falls, and seldome vaine:

Whether some kinder Powers that wish us well,
What they above can not prevent, foretell;
Or the great World do by consent presage,
As hollow Seas with future Tempests rage:
Or rather *Heav'n*, which us so long foresees,
Their fun'ralls celebrates while it decrees.
But never yet was any humane Fate
By nature solemniz'd with so much state.
He unconcern'd the dreadful passage crost;
But oh what Pangs that Death did Nature cost!
  First the great Thunder was shot off and sent,
The signall from the starry Battlement:
The Winds receive it and its force out do,
As practising how they could thunder too;
Out of the Binders Hand the Sheaves they tore,
And thrash'd the Harvest in the airy floore;
Or of huge Trees, whose growth with his did rise,
The deep foundations open'd to the Skyes.
Then heavy Showres the winged Tempests lead
And powre the deluge ore the Chaos head.
The Race of warlike Horses at his Tombe
Offer themselves in many a Hecatombe;
With pensive head towards the grounde they fall,
And helpless languish at the tainted Stall.
Numbers of men decrease with pains unknown,
And hasten, not to see his Death, their own.
Such Tortures all the Elements unfix'd,

Troubled to part where so exactly mixd:
And as through Aire his wasting Spirits flow'd,
The Universe labour'd beneath their load.

   Nature it seem'd with him would Nature vye;
He with *Eliza*, it with him would dye.

   He without noyse still travell'd to his End,
As silent Sunns to meet the Night descend.
The Starrs that for him fought had only power
Left to determine now his fatall Houre;
Which, since they might not hinder, yet they cast
To choose it worthy of his Gloryes past.

   No part of time but bare his marke away
Of honour, all the year was *Cromwell's* day,
But this, of all the most auspicious found,
Twice had in open feild him Victour crownd:
When up the armed Mountains of *Dunbarre*
He march'd, and through deep *Severn* ending warre.
What day should him eternize but the same
That had before immortaliz'd his Name?
That so who ere would at his death have joyd,
In their own Griefs might find themselves imployd;
But those that sadly his departure griev'd,
Yet joy'd remembring what he once atchiev'd.
And the last minute his victorious Ghost
Gave chase to *Ligny* on the *Belgick* coast.
Here ended all his mortal toyles; he layd
And slept in peace under the Laurell shade.

O *Cromwell, Heavens Favourite*! To none
Have such high honours from above been showne:
For whom the Elements we Mourners see,
And *Heav'n* it selfe would the great Herald be;
Which with more Care set forth his Obsequyes
Than those of *Moses* hid from humane Eyes:
As jealous onely here lest all be lesse,
That we could to his Memory expresse.

   Then let us too our course of Mourning keep:
Where *Heaven* leads, 'tis Piety to weep.
Stand back, ye Seas, and shrunck beneath the vaile
Of your Abisse, with cover'd Head bewaile
Your *Monarch*: We demand not your supplyes
To compass in our *Isle*; our Teares suffice;
Since him away the dismall Tempest rent,
Who once more joyn'd us to the Continent;
Who planted *England* on the *Flandrick* shore,
And stretch'd our frontire to the *Indian* Ore;
Whose greater Truths obscure the Fables old:
Whether of *British Saints* or *Worthyes* told;
And in a Valour less'ning *Arthur's* deeds,
For Holinesse the *Confessour* exceeds.

   He first put Armes into *Religion's* hand,
And tim'rous *Conscience* unto *Courage* mann'd;
The soldier taught that inward Maile to weare,
And *fearing God* how they should *nothing feare*.
Those strokes, he said, will pierce through all below

Where those that strike from *Heaven* fetch their Blow.
Astonish'd Armyes did their Flight prepare:
And Cityes strong were stormed by his Prayer.
Of that for ever *Prestons* field shall tell
The story, and impregnable *Clonmell*;
And where the sandy mountain *Fenwick* scal'd,
The Sea between, yet hence his Pray'r prevail'd.
What man was ever so in *Heav'n* obey'd
Since the commanded Sun ore *Gibeon* stayd?
In all his Warrs needs must he triumph, when
He conquer'd *God* still ere he fought with *Men*.

   Hence, though in Battle none so brave or fierce,
Yet him the adverse Steel could never pierce:
Pitty it seem'd to hurt him more that felt
Each Wound himself which he to others delt;
Danger it self refusing to offend
So loose an Enemy, so fast a Friend.

   Friendship, that sacred vertue, long does claime
The first foundation of his House and Name:
But within one its narrow limitts fall;
His Tendernesse extended unto all:
And that deep Soule through every chanell flows,
Where kindly Nature loves it self to lose.
More strong affections never Reason serv'd
Yet still affected most what best deserv'd.
If he *Eliza* lov'd to that degree
(Though who more worthy to be lov'd than she?)

If so indulgent to his own, how deare
To him the Children of the *Highest* were?
For her he once did Natures tribute pay:
For these his Life adventur'd every day.
And 'twould be found, could we his thoughts have cast,
Their Griefs struck deepest, if *Eliza's* last.

What Prudence more than humane did he need
To keep so deare, so diff'ring mindes agreed?
The worser sort, as conscious of their ill,
Lye weak and easy to the Rulers will:
But to the good (too many or too few),
All Law is uselesse, all reward is due.
Oh ill advis'd if, not for love, for shame!
Spare yet your own if you neglect his Fame,
Lest others dare to think your Zeale a maske,
And you to govern only *Heavens* taske.

Valour, Religion, Friendship, Prudence dy'd
At once with him and all that's good beside:
And we, Deaths reffuse, Natures dregs, confin'd
To loathsome life, Alas! are left behinde,
Where we (so once we us'd) shall now no more
To fetch day presse about his Chamber Door;
From which he issu'd with that awfull State,
It seem'd *Mars* broke through *Janus* double Gate:
Yet always temper'd with an Aire so mild,
No Aprill Suns that ere so gently smil'd;
No more shall heare that powerfull Language charm,

Whose force oft spar'd the labour of his arm;
No more shall follow where he spent the dayes
In warre, in counsell, or in pray'r, and praise,
Whose meanest Acts he would himself advance,
As ungirt *David* to the *Arke* did dance.
All, All is gone of ours or his delight
In Horses fierce, wild Deer or Armour bright.
Francisca faire can nothing now but weep,
Nor with soft Notes shall sing his Cares asleep.

   I saw him dead, a leaden Slumber lyes,
And mortall Sleep, over those wakefull Eys:
Those gentle Rayes under the lidds were fled
Which through his lookes that piercing Sweetnesse
     shed;
That Port which so Majestique was and strong,
Loose, and depriv'd of Vigour, stretch'd along:
All wither'd, all discolour'd, pale and wan,
How much another thing, no more than Man?
Oh humane Glory vaine, Oh Death, Oh Wings,
Oh worthless World, oh transitory Things!

   Yet dwelt that Greatnesse in his shape decay'd
That still, though dead, greater than death he layd.
And in his alter'd face you something faigne
That threatens Death he yet will live againe:
Not much unlike the sacred Oake which shoots
To heav'n its branches and through earth its roots,
Whose spacious boughs are hung with Trophees round,

And honour'd wreaths have oft the Victour crown'd.
When angry *Jove* darts Lightning through the Aire
At mortalls sins, nor his own Plant will spare
(It groanes and bruses all below that stood
So many yeares the shelter of the wood),
The tree, ere while foreshorten'd to our view,
When faln shews taller yet than as it grew.

So shall his Praise to after times increase,
When Truth shall be allow'd and Faction cease,
And his own shadows with him fall. The Eye
Detracts from objects than it selfe more high:
But when Death takes them from that envy'd seate,
Seeing how little, we confesse how greate.

Thee many ages hence in martiall Verse
Shall *th' English* Souldier, 'ere he charge, rehearse:
Singing of thee, inflame themselves to fight,
And with the name of *Cromwell* Armyes fright.
As long as Rivers to the Seas shall runne,
As long as *Cynthia* shall relieve the Sunne,
While Staggs shall fly unto the Forests thick,
While Sheep delight the grassy Downs to pick,
As long as Future Time succeeds the Past,
Always thy Honour, Praise and Name shall last.

Thou in a pitch how farre beyond the sphere
Of humane Glory towr'st, and, raigning there,
Despoyld of mortall robes, in seas of Blisse
Plunging dost bathe, and tread a bright Abysse:

There thy greate soule yet once a world does see
Spacious enough and pure enough for thee.
How soon thou *Moses* hast and *Joshua* found
And *David* for the Sword and harpe renown'd!
How streight canst to each happy Mansion goe!
(Farr better known above than here below)
And in these joyes dost spend the endlesse Day
Which in expressing we our selves betray.

    For we, since thou art gone, with heavy Doome
Wander like Ghosts about thy loved Tombe,
And lost in tears have neither sight nor minde
To guide us upward through this Region blinde.
Since thou art gone, who best that Way could'st teach,
Onely our Sighs perhaps may thither reach.

    And *Richard* yet, where his great *Parent* led,
Beats on the rugged track: he Vertue dead
Revives, and by his milder beams assures,
And yet how much of them his griefe obscures?

    He, as his Father, long was kept from sight,
In private to be view'd by better light;
But open'd once, what splendour does he throw:
A *Cromwell* in an houre a Prince will grow!
How he becomes that Seat, how strongly streins,
How gently winds at once the ruling Reins!
Heav'n to this choise prepar'd a Diadem
Richer than any Eastern silk or gemme:
A pearly rainbow, where the Sun inchas'd

His brows like an Imperiall Jewell grac'd.
    We find already what those Omens mean,
Earth nere more glad, nor *Heaven* more serene:
Cease now our griefs, Calme Peace succeeds a War;
Rainbows to storms, *Richard* to *Oliver*.
Tempt not his Clemency to try his pow'r,
He threats no Deluge, yet foretells a Showre.

THE SECOND ADVICE TO A PAINTER
FOR DRAWING THE HISTORY OF OUR
NAVALL BUSYNESSE. IN IMITATION OF
MR. *WALLER*

Navem si poscat sibi peronatus arator
Luciferi rudis, exclamet Melicerta perisse
Frontem de rebus.

                                   Pers: Sat. 5.

London, Aprill 1666
    Nay *Painter*, if thou dar'st designe that Fight
Which *Waller* only Courage had to write;
If thy bold hand can without shaking draw
What ev'n the Actors trembled when they saw;
Enough to make thy colours change, like theirs,
And all thy Pencills bristle like their haires;
First, in fit distance of the Prospect vain,
Paint *Allen* tilting at the coast of *Spain*:
Heroick act, and never heard till now,
Stemming of *Herc'les Pillars* with his Prow!
And how two Ships he left the Hills to waft
And with new Sea-marks *Dov'r* and *Calais* graft;
Next, let the flaming *London* come in view
Like *Nero's Rome*, burnt to rebuild it new.
What lesser Sacrifice than this was meet
To offer for the safety of the Fleet?

Blow one Ship up, another thence does grow:
See what free Cityes and wise Courts can do!
So some old Merchant, to ensure his Name
Marries afresh, and Courtiers share the Dame.
So whatsoere is broke the Servants pay't;
And Glasses are more durable than Plate.
No May'r till now so rich a Pageant feign'd,
Nor one Barge all the Companyes contain'd.

    Then, *Painter*, draw cerulean *Coventry*,
Keeper, or rather Chanc'lour of the Sea:
And more exactly to expresse his hew,
Use nothing but ultramarinish blew.
To pay his Fees the silver Trumpet spends:
And Boatswains whistle for his Place depends:
Pilots in vain repeat the Compasse ore
Untill of him they learn that one point more.
The constant Magnet to the Pole does hold,
Steele to the Magnet, *Coventry* to Gold.
Muscovy sells up hemp and pitch and tarre;
Iron and copper *Sweden*, *Münster* Warre,
Ashley, prize, Warwick, customs, Cart'ret, pay;
But Coventry sells the whole Fleet away.

    Now let our navy stretch its canvas Wings
Swoln like his Purse, with tackling like its strings,
By slow degrees of the increasing gaile,
First under Sale, and after under Saile.
Then, in kind visit unto *Opdams* Gout,

Hedge the *Dutch* in only to let them out.
(So Huntsmen faire unto the Hares give Law,
First find them, and then civilly withdraw)
That the blind *Archer*, when they take the Seas,
The Hamburgh Convoy may betray at ease.
(So that the fish may more securely bite
The Fisher baits the River over night.)
  But *Painter* now prepare, t'inrich thy Piece,
Pencill of Ermins, Oyle of Ambergris.
See where the *Dutchesse*, with triumphant taile
Of num'rous Coaches *Harwich* does assaile.
So the Land-Crabbs at Natures kindly call,
Down to engender at the Sea do crawle.
See then the Admirall, with navy whole
To Harwich through the Ocean caracole.
So Swallows bury'd in the Sea, at Spring
Returne to Land with Summer in their Wing.
  One thrifty Ferry-boat of Mother-Pearl
Suffic'd of old the *Cytherean Girle*.
Yet Navys are but Properties when here,
A small Sea-masque, and built to court you, Dear;
Three Goddesses in one: *Pallas* for Art,
Venus for sport, and *Juno* in your Heart.
  O *Dutchesse*, if thy nuptiall Pomp were mean,
Tis payd with intrest in this navall Scene!
Never did *Roman Mark*, within the *Nile*,
So feast the faire *Egiptian Crocodile*,

Nor the *Venetian Duke*, with such a State,
The *Adriatick* marry at that rate.

　　Now, *Painter*, spare thy weaker art, forbear
To draw her parting Passions and each Tear;
For Love, alas, has but a short delight:
The Winds, the *Dutch*, the *King*, all call to fight.
She therefore the *Dukes* person recommends
To *Bronkard*, *Pen*, and *Coventry*, as Freinds:
(*Pen* much, more *Bronkard*, most to *Coventry*)
For they, she knew, were all more 'fraid than shee.

　　Of flying Fishes one had sav'd the finne,
And hop'd with these he through the Aire might spinne,
The other thought he might avoid his Knell
In the invention of the diving Bell,
The third had try'd it and affirm'd a Cable
Coyl'd round about men was impenetrable.
But these the *Duke* rejected, only chose
To keep far off, and others interpose.

　　Rupert, that knew not fear but health did want,
Kept State suspended in a *Chais-volant*.
All, save his head, shut in that wooden case,
He show'd but like a broken Weather-glasse:
But arm'd in a whole Lion Cap-a-chin,
Did represent the *Hercules* within.
Dear shall the *Dutch* his twinging anguish know
And feele what Valour, whet with Pain, can do.
Curst in the mean time be the Traitresse *Jael*

That through his Princely Temples drove the Naile.
    Rupert resolv'd to fight it like a Lyon.
But *Sandwich* hop'd to fight it like *Arion*:
He, to prolong his Life in the dispute,
And charm the *Holland* Pirats, tun'd his Lute:
Till some judicious Dolphin might approach,
And land him safe and sound as any Roach.

    Now *Painter* reassume thy Pencill's care,
It hath but skirmisht yet, now Fight prepare,
And draw the Battell terribler to show
Than the *Last Judgment* was of *Angelo*.

    First, let our Navy scowr through Silver Froath,
The Ocean's burthen, and the Kingdomes both:
Whose ev'ry Bulk may represent its Birth
From *Hide*, and *Paston*, Burthens of the Earth:
Hide, whose transcendent Paunch so swells of late,
That he the Rupture seems of Law, and State;
Paston, whose Belly bears more Millions
Than *Indian* Caricks, and contains more Tunns.

    Let sholes of Porpisses on evry side
Wonder in swimming by our Oakes outvy'd:
And the Sea Fowle at gaze behold a thing
So vast, more strong, and swift than they of Wing:
But with presaging Gorge yet keep in sight,
And follow for the Relicks of a Fight.

    Then let the *Dutch* with well dissembled Fear
Or bold Despaire, more than we wish draw near.

At which our Gallants, to the Sea but tender,
And more to fight, their easy Stomachs render:
With Breast so panting that at evry stroke
You might have felt their Hearts beat through the Oake.
While one, concern'd most, in the intervall
Of straining Choler, thus did cast his Gall.

    "*Noah* be damn'd and all his Race accurst,
That in Sea brine did pickle Timber first.
What though he planted Vines! he Pines cut down.
He taught us how to drink, and how to drown.
He first built ships, and in the wooden Wall
Saving but Eight, ere since indangers all.
And thou *Dutch* necromantic Friar, damn'd
And in thine own first Mortar-piece be ram'd,
Who first inventedst Cannon in thy Cell,
Nitre from Earth, and Brimstone fetcht from hell,
But damn'd and treble damn'd be *Clarendine*
Our Seventh *Edward* and his House and Line,
Who, to divert the danger of the Warre
With *Bristoll*, hounds us on the *Hollander*;
Foole-coated Gown-man, sells, to fight with *Hans*,
Dunkirk; dismantling *Scotland*, quarrels *France*,
And hopes he now hath bus'nesse shap't and Pow'r
T'outlast his Life or ours, and scape the *Tow'r*:
And that he yet may see, ere he go down,
His dear *Clarinda* circled in a Crown."

    By this time both the Fleets in reach debute

And each the other mortally salute.
Draw pensive *Neptune* biting of his Thumms,
To think himself a Slave whos'ere orecomes,
The frighted Nymphs retreating to the Rocks,
Beating their blew Breasts, tearing their green Locks;
Paint *Echo* slain: only th' alternate Sound
From the repeating Canon does rebound.

    Opdam sailes in, plac'd in his navall Throne,
Assuming Courage greater than his own;
Makes to the *Duke*, and threatens him from farr
To naile himself to's Board like a Petarre:
But in the vain attempt takes Fire too soon,
And flyes up in his Ship to catch the Moon.
Monsieurs like Rockets mount aloft, and crack
In thousand Sparks, then dansingly fall back.

    Yet ere this happen'd Destiny allow'd
Him his Revenge, to make his Death more proud.
A fatall Bullet from his Side did range,
And batter'd *Lawson*, O too dear Exchange!
He led our Fleet that Day, too short a Space,
But lost his Knee, (dy'd since) in Gloryes Race,
Lawson, whose Valour beyond Fate did go
And still fights *Opdam* through the Lakes below.

    The *Duke* himself, though *Pen* did not forget,
Yet was not out of dangers random set.
Falmouth was there, I know not what to act
(Some say 'twas to grow Duke too by Contact.)

An untaught Bullet in its wanton Scope
Quashes him all to pieces, and his Hope.
Such as his Rise such was his Fall, unprais'd;
A Chance-shot sooner took than Chance him rais'd:
His Shatterd Head the fearlesse *Duke* distains,
And gave the last first proof that he had Brains.

   Barkley had heard it soon, and thought not good
To venture more of Royall *Harding's* Blood.
To be immortall he was not of Age
(And did ev'n now the *Indian* Prize presage),
But judg'd it safe and decent, cost what cost,
To lose the Day, since his Dear Brother's lost.
With his whole Squadron streight away he bore
And, like good Boy, promist to fight no more.

   The *Dutch Urania* carelesse at us saild,
And promises to do what *Opdam* faild.
Smith to the *Duke* does intercept her Way
And cleaves t' her closer than the *Remora*.
The Captaine wonder'd, and withall disdain'd
So strongly by a thing so small detain'd:
And in a raging Brav'ry to him runs.
They stab their Ships with one anothers Guns,
They fight so near it seems to be on Ground,
And ev'n the Bullets meeting Bullets wound.
The Noise, the Smoak, the Sweat, the Fire, the Blood
Is not to be exprest nor understood.
Each Captaine from the Quarter-deck commands,

They wave their bright Swords glitt'ring in their hands;
All Luxury of Warre, all Man can do
In a Sea-fight, did passe betwixt them two.
But one must conquer whosoever fight:
Smith tooke the Giant, and is since made Knight.
    Marleburgh, that knew and dar'd too more than all,
Falls undistinguisht by an Iron Ball.
Dear Lord, but born under a Starre ingrate!
No Soule so clear, and no more gloomy Fate.
Who would set up Warr's Trade that meant to thrive?
Death picks the Valiant out, the Cow'rds survive.
What the Brave merit th' Impudent do vaunt,
And none's rewarded but the Sycophant.
Hence, all his Life he against Fortune fenc'd;
Or not well known, or not well recompens'd.
But envy not this Praise to's Memory:
None more prepar'd was or lesse fit to dye.
    Rupert did others and himself excell:
Holmes, Teddyman, Minns; bravely *Samson* fell.
What others did let none omitted blame:
I shall record whos'ere brings in his Name.
But unlesse after Storyes disagree,
Nine onely came to fight, the rest to see.
    Now all conspires unto the Dutchmen's Losse:
The Wind, the Fire, we, they themselves do crosse.
When a Sweet Sleep the *Duke* began to drown,
And with soft Diadem his Temples crown.

But first he orders all beside to watch;
And they the Foe while he a Nap should catch.

But *Bronkard*, by a secreter instinct,
Slept not, nor needs it; he all Day had wink't.
The *Duke* in Bed, he then first draws his Steele,
Whose Virtue makes the misled Compasse wheele:
So ere he wak'd, both Fleets were innocent,
And *Bronkard* Member is of Parliament.

And now, dear *Painter*, after pains like those
'Twere time that thou and I too should repose.
But all our Navy scap'd so sound of Limm
That a small space serv'd to refresh its trimm.
And a tame Fleet of theirs does Convoy want,
Laden with both the *Indyes* and *Levant*.
Paint but this one Scene more, the world's our own:
The *Halcyon Sandwich* does command alone.

To *Bergen* now with better Maw we haste,
And the sweet spoyles in Hope already taste,
Though *Clifford* in the Character appears
Of *Supracargo* to our Fleet and theirs,
Wearing a signet ready to clap on,
And seize all for his Master, *Arlington*.

Ruyter, whose little Squadron skim'd the Seas
And wasted our remotest Colonyes,
With Ships all foule return'd upon our Way;
Sandwich would not disperse, nor yet delay,
And therefore, like Commander grave and wise,

To scape his Sight and Fight, shut both his Eyes,
And, for more State and surenesse, *Cuttins* true
The left Eye closes, the right *Montague*,
And even *Clifford* profer'd, in his Zeale
To make all safe, t'apply to both his Seale.
Ulisses so, till he the *Syrens* past,
Would by his Mates be pinion'd to the Mast.

    Now may our Navy view the wished Port
But there too (see the Fortune!) was a Fort.
Sandwich would not be beaten, nor yet beat:
Fooles only fight, the Prudent use to treat.
His Cousin *Montague*, by Court disaster
Dwindled into the wooden Horse's Master,
To speak of Peace seem'd among all most proper,
Had *Talbot* then treated of nought but Copper,
For what are Forts when void of Ammunition?
With Freind or Foe what would we more condition?
Yet we three dayes, till the *Dutch* furnish all –
Men, Powder, Cannon, Money – treat with *Wall*.
Then *Teddy*, finding that the *Dane* would not,
Sends in Six Captains bravely to be shot.
And *Montague*, though drest like any Bride,
Though aboard him too, yet was reacht and dy'd.

    Sad was this Chance, and yet a deeper Care
Wrinkles our Membranes under Forehead faire.
The *Dutch Armada* yet had th' Impudence
To put to Sea, to waft their Merchants hence.

For, as if all their Ships of Wall-nut were,
The more we beat them, still the more they bear.
But a good Pilot and a fav'ring Winde
Bring *Sandwich* back, and once again did blind.

Now gentle *Painter*, ere we leap on Shore,
With thy last strokes ruffle a Tempest o'er:
As if in our Reproach, the Winds and Seas
Would undertake the *Dutch* while we take Ease,
The Seas their Spoiles within our Hatches throw,
The Winds both Fleets into our Mouthes do blow,
Strew all their Ships along the Coast by ours,
As easy to be gather'd up as Flow'rs.
But *Sandwich* fears for Merchants to mistake
A Man of Warre, and among Flow'rs a Snake.
Two *Indian* Ships pregnant with Eastern Pearle
And Di'monds sate the Officers and *Earle*;
Then warning of our Fleet, he it divides
Into the Ports, and he to *Oxford* rides,
While the *Dutch* reuniting, to our Shames,
Ride all insulting o'er the *Downs* and *Thames*.

Now treating *Sandwich* seems the fittest choice
For *Spain*, there to condole and to rejoyce.
He meets the *French*, but, to avoyd all harms,
Slips to the *Groyne* (Embassyes bear not Arms!)
There let him languish a long *Quarantain*,
And ne'er to *England* come till he be clean.

Thus having fought we know not why, as yet,

We've done we know not what, nor what we get.
If to espouse the Ocean all this paines,
Princes unite and will forbid the Baines;
If to discharge Fanaticks, this makes more,
For all Fanatick turn when sick or poore;
Or if the *House of Commons* to repay,
Their Prize Commissions are transfer'd away;
But for triumphant Checkstones, if, and Shell
For *Dutchesse'* Closet, 't has succeeded well.
If to make Parliaments all odious passe,
If to reserve a Standing Force, alas,
Or if, as just, *Orange* to reinstate,
Instead of that, he is regenerate;
And with four Millions vainly giv'n, as spent,
And with five Millions more of detriment,
Our Summe amounts yet only to have won
A Bastard *Orange* for Pimp *Arlington.*

    Now may Historians argue Con and Pro:
Denham saith thus, though *Waller* always so,
But he, good Man, in his long Sheet and Staffe
This Penance did for *Cromwell's* Epitaph.
And his next Theme must be of *th' Duke's Maistress*:
Advice to draw *Madam Edificatresse.*

    Henceforth, O Gemini! two *Dukes* command:
Castor and *Pollux, Aumarle, Cumberland.*
Since in one Ship, it had been fit they went
In *Petty's* double-keel'd *Experiment.*

To the King

    Imperiall *Prince*, King of the Seas and Isles,
Dear Object of our Joys and Heaven's Smiles,
What boots it that thy Light does guild our Dayes
And we lye basking by thy milder Rayes,
While Swarms of Insects, from thy warmth begun,
Our Land devour, and intercept our Sunn?
    Thou, like *Jove's Minos*, rul'st a greater *Crete*
(And for its hundred Cityes count thy Fleet.)
Why wilt thou that *State-Dedalus* allow,
Who builds thee but a Lab'rinth and a Cow?
If thou art *Minos*, be a Judge Severe,
And in's own Maze confine the Engineer,
Or if our Sunn, since he so near presumes,
Melt the soft wax with which he imps his Plumes,
And let him falling leave his hated Name
Unto those Seas his Warre bath set on Flame.
From that Enchanter having clear'd thine Eyes,
Thy Native Sight will pierce within the Skyes,
And view those Kingdomes calm of Joy and Light
Where's universall Triumph but no Fight,
Since both from Heav'n thy Race and Pow'r descend,
Rule by its pattern, there to reascend.
Let Justice only draw: and Battell cease.
Kings are in War but Cards: they're Gods in Peace.

THE LAST INSTRUCTIONS TO A PAINTER
London. September 4th, 1667

After two sittings, now, our Lady State,
To end her Picture, does the third time waite.
But ere thou falst to worke, first, *Painter*, see
It be'nt too slight grown or too hard for thee.
Canst thou paint without colors? Then 'tis right:
For so wee too without a Fleet can fight.
Or canst thou dawb a sign-post, and that ill?
'Twill suit our great debauch and little skill.
Or hast thou mark'd how antique Masters limn
The Aly roof with Snuffe of Candle dimme,
Sketching in shady smoke prodigious tooles?
'Twill serve this race of Drunkards, Pimps, and Fooles.
But if to match our crimes thy skill presumes,
As *th' Indians*, draw our Luxury in Plumes;
Or if to score out our compendious Fame,
With *Hooke*, then, through the *Microscope* take aim,
Where, like the new *Controller*, all men laugh
To see a tall Lowse brandish the white staffe.
Else shalt thou oft thy guiltlesse Pencill curse,
Stamp on thy Pallat, nor perhaps the worse.
The Painter so, long having vext his cloth,
Of his Hound's mouth to feign the raging froth,
His desp'rate Pencill at the work did dart:
His Anger reacht that rage which past his Art;

Chance finisht that which Art could but begin,
And he sat smiling how his Dog did grin.
So mayst thou perfect, by a lucky blow,
What all thy softest touches can not do.

    Paint then *St. Albans*, full of soup and gold,
The new *Court's* patern, Stallion of the old.
Him neither Wit nor Courage did exalt,
But Fortune chose him for her pleasure Salt.
Paint him with Dray-man's shoulders, Butcher's Mien,
Member'd like Mules, with elephantine Chine.
Well he the title of *St. Albans* bore,
For *Bacon* never study'd Nature more.
But Age, allaying now that youthful heat,
Fits him in *France* to play at Cards and treat.
Draw no Commission, lest the *Court* should lie,
That disavowing Treaty asks supply.
He needs no Seale, but to *St. James's* Lease,
Whose briches wear the Instrument of Peace;
Who, if the *French* dispute his Pow'r, from thence
Can streight produce them a Plenipotence.
Nor fears he *The most Christian* should trepan
Two Saints at once, *St. Germain*, *St. Alban*,
But thought the golden Age was now restor'd,
When Men and Women took each others Word.

    Paint then again *Her Highnesse* to the life,
Philosopher beyond *Newcastle's* Wife.
She, nak'd, can *Archimedes* self put down,

For an experiment upon the Crown.
She perfected that Engine, oft assayd,
How after childbirth to renew a Maid,
And found how Royall Heirs might be matur'd
In fewer Months than Mothers once indur'd.
Hence *Crowder* made the rare Inventresse free
Of's *Highnesse's* Royall Society:
Happy'st of Women, if she were but able
To make her glassen *Dukes* once malleable!
Paint her with Oyster lip, and Breath of Fame,
Wide Mouth, that Sparagus may well proclaime:
With *Chanc'lors* Belly, and so large a Rump
There, not behind the Coach, her Pages jump.
Expresse her studying now, if *China* clay
Can without breaking venom'd Juice convay,
Or how a mortall Poyson she may draw
Out of the cordiall meale of the Cacao.
Witnesse, ye starrs of Night, and thou the pale
Moon, that o'recome with the sick steam didst faile;
Ye neighbring Elms, that your green leaves did shed,
And Fawns, that from the Wombe abortive fled!
Not unprovok'd, she trys forbidden Arts,
But in her soft Breast Love's hid Cancer smarts,
While she revolves at once *Sidney's* disgrace
And her self scorn'd for emulous *Denham's* Face.
And nightly hears the hated Guards away
Galloping with the *Duke* to other Prey.

Paint *Castlemain* in Colors that will hold
(Her, not her Picture, for she now grows old).
She through her Lackyes drawers, as he ran,
Discern'd Love's cause, and a new Flame began.
Her wonted Joys, thenceforth, and *Court* she shuns,
And still within her Mind the Footman runs:
His brazen Calves, his brawny Thighs (the Face
She slights), his Feet shap'd for a smoother race.
Poring within her Glasse she readjusts
Her Lookes and oft-try'd Beauty now distrusts;
Fears lest he scorn a Woman once assayd,
And now first wisht she e'er had been a Maid.
Great Love, how dost thou triumph, and how reigne,
That to a Groom couldst humble her disdaine!
Stript to her Skin, see how shee stooping stands,
Nor scorns to rub him down with those faire Hands,
And washing (lest the Scent her Crime disclose)
His sweaty Hooves, tickles him 'twixt the Toes.
But envious Fame, too soon, begun to note
More gold in's fob, more lace upon his coat:
And he unwary, and of Tongue too fleet,
No longer could conceale his Fortune sweet.
Justly the Rogue was whipt in Porters Den,
And *Jermin* streight has leave to come agen.
Ah, *Painter*, now could *Alexander* live,
And this *Campaspe* thee, *Apelles*, give!
    Draw next a Paire of Tables op'ning, then

The *House of Commons* clat'ring like the Men.
Describe the *Court* and *Country*, both set right,
On opposite points, the black against the white:
Those having lost the Nation at Trick-track,
These now advent'ring how to win it back.
The Dice betwixt them must the Fate divide
(As Chance doth still in Multitudes decide).
But here the *Court* does its advantage know,
For the Cheat *Turner* for them both must throw.
As some from Boxes, he so from the Chaire
Can strike the Die and still with them goes share.

   Here, *Painter*, rest a little, and survey
With what small Arts the publick game they play.
For so too *Rubens* with affaires of State
His lab'ring Pencill oft would recreate.

   The close *Caball* markt how the Navy eats
And thought all lost that goes not to the cheats;
So therefore secretly for Peace decrees,
Yet as for Warre the *Parlament* would squeeze,
And fix to the Revenue such a summe
Should *Goodrick* silence, and strike *Paston* dumbe,
Should pay land Armyes, should dissolve the vain
Commons, and ever such a *Court* maintaine;
Hide's Avarice, *Bennet's* Luxury should suffice:
And what can these defray but the *Excise*?
Excise, a Monster worse than ere before,
Frighted the Midwife and the Mother tore.

A thousand Hands she has, and thousand Eyes:
Breks into shops and into Cellars pryes,
With hundred rows of teeth the Sharke exceeds,
And on all trade like Casawar shee feeds:
Chops off the piece wheres'ere she close the Jaw,
Else swallows all down her indented maw.
She stalks all day in Streets conceal'd from sight
And flyes like Batts with leathern wings by night,
She wastes the Country and on Cityes preys:
Her, of a female *Harpy*, in Dog-dayes,
Black *Birch*, of all the earthborn race most hot
And most rapacious, like himself begot,
And, of his Bratt inamour'd, as't increast,
Bougred in incest with the mungrell Beast.

    Say, *Muse*, for nothing can escape thy Sight
(And, *Painter*, wanting other, draw this Fight)
Who in an *English Senate* fierce debate
Could raise so long for this new whore of State.

    Of early Wittalls first the Troop march'd in,
For Diligence renown'd and Discipline:
In loyall haste they left young Wives in Bed,
And *Denham* these by one consent did head.
Of the old Courtiers next a Squadron came,
That sold their *Master*, led by *Ashburnham*.
To them succeeds a despicable Rout,
But know the Word, and well could face about:
Expectants pale, with hopes of Spoyle allur'd,

Though yet but Pioneers, and led by *Stew'rd.*
Then damning Cowards rang'd the vocall Plain:
Wood these commands, Knight of the Horn and Cane.
Still his hook-shoulder seems the blow to dread,
And under's Armpit he defends his Head.
The posture strange men laught at of his Poll,
Hid with his Elbow like the Spice he stole.
Headlesse *St. Dennis* so his Head does beare,
And both of them alike *French Martyrs* were.
Court Officers, as us'd, the next place tooke
And follow'd *Fox*, but with disdainfull looke.
His Birth, his Youth, his Brokage all dispraise,
In vain, for always he commands that payes.
Then the Procurers under *Prodgers* fil'd,
Gentlest of men, and his Lieutenant mild,
Bronkard, Love's squire; through all the field array'd
No Troop was better clad, nor so well pay'd.
Then marcht the Troop of *Clarindon*, all full,
Haters of Fowle, to teale preferring Bull:
Grosse Bodyes, grosser Minds, and grossest cheats,
And bloated *Wrenn* conducts them to their seats.
Charlton advances next, whose coife does aw
The *Miter Troop*, and with his looks gives Law.
He marcht with beaver cockt of Bishop's brimme
And hid much Fraud under an aspect grimme.
Next th' Lawyers mercenary band appeare,
Finch in the Front, and *Thurland* in the reare.

The Troop of Privilege, a Rabble bare
Of Debtors deep, fell to *Trelawny's* care.
Their Fortunes error they supply'd in Rage,
Nor any further would than these ingage.
Then march't the Troop whose valiant Acts before
(Their publick Acts) oblig'd them still to more.
For Chimney's sake they all *Sir Poole* obey'd,
Or in his absence him that first it lay'd.
Then comes the thrifty Troop of Privateers,
Whose Horses each with other interferes:
Before them *Higgons* rides with brow compact,
Mourning his *Countesse*, anxious for his *Act.*
Sir Frederick and *Sir Salomon* draw Lotts
For the command of Politicks or Sotts;
Thence fell to words, but, quarrell to adjourn,
Their freinds agreed they should command by turn.
Cart'ret the rich did the Accountants guide,
And in ill *English* all the World defy'd.
The *Papists,* but of these the *House* had none;
Else *Talbot* offer'd to have led them on.
Bold *Duncom* next, of the Projectors chief:
And old *Fitzharding* of the *Eaters Beef.*
Late and disorder'd out the Drinkers drew;
Scarce them their Leaders, they their Leaders knew.
Before them enter'd, equall in Command,
Apsly and *Brothrick,* marching hand in hand.
Last then but one *Powell,* that could not ride,

Led the *French Standard*, weltring in his stride.
He, to excuse his slownesse, truth confest
That 'twas so long before he could be drest.
The Lords' Sons, last, all these did reinforce:
Cornb'ry before them manag'd Hobby-horse.

   Never, before nor since, a Host so steel'd
Troopt on to muster in the *Tuttle-field*.
Not the first cock-horse that with cork were shod
To rescue *Albermarle* from the Sea-Cod:
Nor the late Feather-men, whom *Tomkins* fierce
Shall with one Breath, like thistle-down disperse.
All the two *Coventrys* their Gen'ralls chose,
For One had much, the other nought to lose;
Nor better choice all accidents could hit,
While *Hector Harry* steers by *Will the Witt*.
They both accept the Charge with merry glee
To fight a Battell from all Gun-shot free.

   Pleas'd with their numbers, yet in Valor wise,
They feigne a Parly better to surprize:
They, that ere long shall the rude *Dutch* upbraid,
Who in a time of Treaty durst invade.

   Thick was the Morning, and the *House* was thin,
The *Speaker* early, when they all fell in.
Propitious *Heavens*, had not you them crost,
Excise had got the Day, and all been lost!
For th' other Side all in loose Quarters lay,
Without Intelligence, Command, or Pay:

A scatter'd Body, which the Foe ne'r try'd,
But oftner did among themselves divide,
And some ran ore each night while others sleep
And undescry'd return'd ere Morning peep.
But *Strangeways*, that all night still walkt the round
(For vigilance and Courage both renown'd)
First spy'd the Enemy and gave th' Alarme:
Fighting it single till the rest might arm.
Such *Roman Cocles* strid: before, the Foe;
The falling Bridge behind, the Stream below.
Each ran, as Chance him guides, to sev'rall Post,
And all to patern his Example boast.
Their former Trophies they recall to mind,
And to new edge their angry Courage grind.
First enter'd forward *Temple*, Conqueror
Of *Irish* Cattell and *Sollicitor*;
Then daring *Seymor*, that with Spear and Shield
Had stretcht the monster *Patent* on the field;
Keen *Whorwood* next, in aid of Damsell fraile,
That pierc't the Gyant *Mordant* through his Maile,
And surly *Williams*, the Accountants bane,
And *Lovelace* young, of Chimney men the Cane.
Old *Waller*, Trumpet-gen'rall, swore he'd write
This Combat truer than the navall Fight.
Of Birth, State, Wit, Strength, Courage, *How'rd*
     presumes
And in his Breast wears many *Montezumes*.

These and some more with single Valor stay
The adverse troops and hold them all at bay.
Each thinks his person represents the whole,
And with that thought does multiply his Soule,
Believes himself an Army, theirs one Man,
As eas'ly conquer'd, and believing, can;
With Heart of Bees so full, and Head of Mites,
That each, though duelling, a Battell fights.
Such once *Orlando*, famous in Romance,
Broach't whole Brigades like Larks upon his Lance.

   But strength at last still under Number bows,
And the faint sweat trickled down *Temple's* Brows.
Ev'n iron *Strangeways*, chafing, yet gave back,
Spent with Fatigue, to breath a while Toback.
When, marching in, a seas'nable Recruit
Of Citizens and Merchants held dispute;
And, charging all their pikes, a sullen Band
Of *Presbyterian Switzers* made a Stand.

   Nor could all these the Field have long maintain'd
But for th' unknown Reserve that still remain'd:
A grosse of *English* Gentry, nobly born,
Of clear Estates, and to no Faction sworn;
Dear Lovers of their *King*, and Death to meet
For Countryes Cause that glorious think and sweet;
To speak not forward, but in Action brave,
In giving gen'rous, but in Counsell grave;
Candidly credulous for once, nay twice,

But sure the *Devill* can not cheat them thrice.
The Van and Battell, though retiring, falls
Without disorder in their Intervalls,
Then, closing all in equall Front, fall on,
Led by great *Garway* and great *Littleton*.
Lee, ready to obey or to command,
Adjutant-Generall was still at hand.
The martiall standard, *Sands* displaying, shows
St. *Dunstan* in it tweaking *Satan's* Nose.
See sudden chance of Warre! To paint or write
Is longer Work and harder than to fight.
At the first Charge the Enemy give out
And the *Excise* receives a totall Rout.

Broken in Courage, yet the Men the same,
Resolve henceforth upon their other Game:
Where force had fail'd, with Stratagem to play,
And what Haste lost recover by Delay.
St. *Albans* streight is sent to, to forbeare,
Lest the sure Peace forsooth too soon appear.
The Seamen's clamour to three ends they use:
To cheat their Pay, feigne want, the *House* accuse.
Each day they bring the Tale, and that too true,
How strong the *Dutch* their Equipage renew.
Mean time through all the Yards their Orders run
To lay the Ships up, cease the keels begun.
The Timber rots, and uselesse Ax doth rust,
Th' unpractis'd Saw lyes bury'd in its Dust;

The busy Hammer sleeps, the Ropes untwine;
The Stores and Wages all are Mine and Thine.
Along the Coast and Harbors they take care
That Money lack, nor Forts be in repaire.
Long thus they could against the *House* conspire,
Load them with Envy, and with Sitting tire:
And the lov'd *King*, and never yet deny'd,
Is brought to beg in publick and to chide.
But when this fail'd, and Months enow were spent,
They with the first dayes proffer seem content:
And to Land-tax from the *Excise* turn round,
Bought off with Eighteen-hundred-thousand pound.
Thus like faire Thieves, the *Commons* purse they share,
But all the Members' Lives consulting spare.

 Blither than Hare that hath escap'd the hounds,
The *House* prorogu'd, the *Chancellor* rebounds.
Not so decrepit Æson, hasht and stew'd
With bitter Herbs, rose from the Pot renew'd,
And with fresh Age felt his glad limms unite.
His Gout (yet still he curst) had left him quite.
What Frosts to Fruit, what Ars'nick to the Rat,
What to faire *Denham* mortall Chocolat,
What an Account to *Cart'ret*, that, and more,
A *Parliament* is to the *Chancellor*.
So the sad tree shrinks from the Morning's Eye,
But blooms all night and shoots its branches high.
So, at the Sun's recesse, againe returns

The Comet dread, and Earth and Heaven burns.
   Now *Mordant* may within his Castle tow'r
Imprison Parents, and the Child deflowre.
The *Irish* herd is now let loose, and comes
By millions over, not by *hecatombs*.
And now, now, the *Canary Patent* may
Be broacht againe for the great Holy-Day.
   See how he reigns in her new Palace culminant,
And sits in state divine like *Jove* the fulminant!
First *Buckingham*, that durst to him rebell,
Blasted with Lightning, struck with Thunder fell.
Next the twelve *Commons* are condemn'd to grone,
And roule in vain at *Sisyphus's* Stone.
But still he car'd, while in Revenge he brav'd,
That Peace secur'd and Money might be sav'd;
Gain and Revenge, Revenge and Gain are sweet:
United most, else when by turns they meet.
France had *St. Albans* promis'd (so they sing),
St. Albans promis'd him, and he the *King*.
The Count forthwith is order'd all to close,
To play for *Flanders* and the stake to lose,
While, chain'd together, two Ambassadors
Like Slaves shall beg for Peace at *Holland's* doores.
This done, among his *Cyclopes* he retires
To forge new Thunder and inspect their Fires.
   The *Court*, as once of War, now fond of Peace,
All to new sports their wanton fears release.

From *Greenwich* (where Intelligence they hold)
Comes News of pastime martiall and old:
A Punishment invented first to aw
Masculine Wives, transgressing Natures Law,
Where, when the brawny Female disobeys,
And beats the Husband till for peace he prays,
No concern'd Jury for him damage finds,
Nor partiall Justice her Behaviour binds,
But the just Street does the next House invade,
Mounting the neighbor Couple on lean Jade;
The Distaffe knocks, the grains from Kettle fly,
And Boys and Girls in Troops run hooting by.
Prudent Antiquity, that knew by Shame,
Better than Law, domestick Crimes to tame,
And taught Youth by Spectacle innocent!
So thou and I, Dear *Painter*, represent,
In quick effigie, others faults, and feigne,
By making them redic'lous, to restraine.
With homely sight, they chose thus to relax
The joys of State for the new Peace and Tax.
So *Holland* with us had the Mast'ry try'd,
And our next neighbors, *France* and *Flanders*, ride.
  But a fresh News, the great designment nips:
Off at the *Isle of Candy, Dutch* and Ships!
Bab May and *Arlington* did wisely scoffe,
And thought all safe if they were so far off:
Modern Geographers, 'twas there, they thought,

Where *Venice* twenty years the *Turk* had fought;
While the first Year our Navy is but shown,
The next divided, and the third we've none.
They, by the Name, mistook it for that Isle
Where *Pilgrim Palmer* travel'd in exile,
With the Bulls horn to measure his own head,
And on *Pasiphäe's* Tombe to drop a Bead.
But *Morrice* learn'd demonstrates, by the Post,
This *Isle of Candy* was on *Essex* Coast.

   Fresh Messengers still the sad News assure,
More tim'rous now we are, than first secure.
False terrors our believing Fears devise:
And the *French* Army one from *Calais* spyes.
Bennet and *May* and those of shorter reach
Change all for Guinnies, and a Crown for each;
But wiser Men, and well foreseen in chance,
In *Holland* theirs had lodg'd before, and *France.*
Whitehall's unsafe, the *Court* all meditates
To fly to *Windsor*, and mure up the Gates.
Each does the other blame, and all distrust;
But *Mordant*, new oblig'd, would sure be just.
Not such a fatall stupefaction reign'd
At *Londons* Flame, nor so the *Court* complain'd.
The *Bloodworth-Chanc'lor* gives, then does recall,
Orders; amaz'd at last gives none at all.

   St. Alban's writ to that he may bewaile
To *Master Lewis*, and tell coward tale,

How yet the *Hollanders* do make a noise,
Threaten to beat us, and are naughty Boyes.
Now *Doleman's* disobedient, and they still
Uncivill; his unkindnesse would us kill.
Tell him our Ships unrigg'd, our Forts unman'd,
Our Money spent; else 'twere at his command.
Summon him therefore of his Word, and prove
To move him out of Pity, if not Love.
Pray him to make *De Witte* and *Ruyter* cease,
And whip the *Dutch* unlesse they'll hold their peace.
But *Lewis* was of memory but dull,
And to *St. Albans* too undutyfull;
Nor Word nor near relation did revere:
But askt him bluntly for his Character.
The Gravell'd *Count* did with the Answer faint
(His Character was that which thou didst paint)
And so inforc'd, like Enemy or Spy,
Trusses his bagage, and the Camp does fly.
Yet *Lewis* writes, and lest our hearts should break,
Consoles us morally out of *Seneque*.

  Two letters next unto *Breda* are sent,
In cipher one to *Harry Excellent*.
The first instructs our (verse the Name abhors)
Plenipotentiary Ambassadors
To prove by Scripture, Treaty does imply
Cessation, as the Look Adultery;
And that, by Law of Arms, in martiall strife,

Who yields his Sword has title to his life.
Presbyter Hollis the first point should cleare;
The second *Coventry* the *Cavalier*.
But would they not be argu'd back from Sea,
Then to return home straight *infectâ re*.
But *Harry's* order'd, if they won't recall
Their Fleet, to threaten, we will grant them all.
The Dutch are then in proclamation shent
For sin against th' eleventh commandment.
Hide's flippant Stile there pleasantly curvets;
Still his sharp Witt on States and Princes whets
(So *Spain* could not escape his Laughter's spleen:
None but himself must choose the King a Queen),
But, when he came the odious clause to pen
That summons up the *Parliament* agen,
His Writing Master many a time he bann'd,
And wisht himself the Gout to seise his Hand.
Never old Leacher more repugnance felt,
Consenting, for his Rupture, to be gelt;
But still in hope he solac't, ere they come,
To work the Peace and so to send them home,
Or in their hasty Fall to find a flaw,
Their Acts to vitiate, and them overaw;
But most rely'd, upon this *Dutch* pretense,
To raise a two edg'd Army for's defense.
    First then he marcht our whole Militia's force
(As if indeed we Ships or *Dutch* had Horse),

Then from the usuall commonplace he blames
These, and in standing Army's praise declames,
And the wise *Court*, that always lov'd it deare,
Now thinks all but too little for their Feare.
Hide stamps, and streight upon the ground the swarms
Of currant *Myrmidons* appear in Arms,
And for their Pay he writes, as from the *King*,
With that curs't quill pluckt from a Vultur's wing,
Of the whole *Nation* now to ask a Loan
(The eighteen-hundred-thousand pound was gone).
      This done, he pens a Proclamation stout
In rescue of the *Banquiers Banquerouts*,
His minion Imps, that, in his secret part,
Ly nuzling at the sacramentall wart;
Horse-leeches circling at the hem'royd veine:
He sucks the *King*, they him, he them againe.
The Kingdomes Farm he lets to them bid least:
Greater the Bribe, and that's at interest.
Here Men, induc'd by safety, gain, and ease,
Their Money lodge, confiscate when he please.
These can at need, at instant, with a scrip,
(This lik'd him best) his Cash beyond Sea whip.
When *Dutch* invade, when *Parliament* prepare,
How can he Engines so convenient spare?
Let no Man touch them or demand his own,
Pain of displeasure of great *Clarindon*.
      The State affaires thus marshal'd, for the rest,

Monk in his shirt against the Dutch is prest.
Often, dear *Painter*, have I sat and mus'd
Why he should still be on all adventures us'd:
If they for nothing ill, like ashen wood,
Or think him, like herbe John, for nothing good?
Whether his Valor they so much admire,
Or that for Cowardise they all retire,
As *Heav'n* in Storms, they call, in gusts of State,
On *Monk* and *Parliament*, yet both do hate.
All Causes sure concurre, but most they think
Under *Herculean* Labors he may sink.
Soon then the independent Troops would close,
And *Hide's* last project would his Place dispose.
    Ruyter the while, that had our Ocean curb'd,
Sail'd now among our Rivers undisturb'd:
Survey'd their chrystall Streams and Banks so green
And Beauties ere this never naked seen.
Through the vain Sedge, the bashfull Nymphs he eyd:
Bosomes and all which from themselves they hide.
The Sun much brighter, and the Skyes more clear,
He finds the Aire and all things sweeter here.
The sudden change and such a tempting Sight
Swells his old Veins with fresh Blood, fresh Delight.
Like am'rous Victors he begins to shave,
And his new Face looks in the *English* wave.
His sporting Navy all about him swim,
And witness their complacence in their Trimme:

230

Their streaming Silks play through the weather fair
And with inveigling colors court the Aire,
While the red Flaggs breathe on their Top-masts high
Terror and War, but want an Enemy.
Among the Shrowds the Seamen sit and sing,
And wanton Boyes on evry Rope do cling.
Old *Neptune* springs the Tides and water lent
(The Gods themselves do help the provident),
And, where the deep keel on the shallow cleaves,
With Trident's leaver and great shoulder heaves.
Æolus their sailes inspires with Eastern wind,
Puffs them along, and breathes upon them kind.
With pearly Shell the *Tritons* all the while
Sound the Sea-march, and guide to *Sheppy Isle.*

   So have I seen, in Aprill's Bud, arise
A Fleet of clouds sailing along the skyes,
The liquid Region with their squadrons fill'd,
Their airy Sterns the Sun behind does guild,
And gentle gales them steere, and *Heaven* drives,
When, all on sudden, their calm bosom rives
With Thund'r and Lightning from each armed Clowd:
Shepheards themselves in vain in bushes shrowd;
Such up the Stream the *Belgick* Navy glides,
And at *Sheernesse* unloads its stormy sides.
Sprag there, though practis'd in the Sea-command,
With panting Heart lay like a Fish on Land
And quickly judg'd the Fort was not tenable,

Which, if a House, yet were not tenantable.
No man can sit there safe: the Canon pours
Thorow the Walls untight and Bullets show'rs,
The neighb'rhood ill, and an unwholsome Seat,
So at the first Salute resolves Retreat
And swore that he would never more dwell there
Untill the *City* put it in repaire;
So he in front, his Garrison in reare,
March streight to *Chatham* to increase the feare.
    There our sick Ships unrigg'd in Summer lay,
Like molting Fowle, a weak and easy Prey.
For whose strong bulk Earth scarce could Timber finde,
The Ocean water, or the Heavens wind
Those Oaken Gyants of the ancient race,
That rul'd all Seas and did our *Chanell* grace.
The conscious Stag, so, once the Forrest's dread,
Flyes to the Wood, and hides his armlesse Head.
Ruyter forthwith a Squadron does untack:
They saile securely through the River's track.
An *English* Pilot too, (O shame, O Sin!)
Cheated of Pay, was he that show'd them in.
Our wretched Ships, within, their Fate attend,
And all our hopes now on fraile Chain depend:
Engine so slight to guard us from the Sea,
It fitter seem'd to captivate a Flea.
A Skipper rude shocks it without respect,
Filling his Sailes, more force to recollect.

Th' *English* from Shore the Iron deaf invoke
For its last aid: "Hold Chain, or we are broke!"
But with her sailing weight the *Holland* keele,
Snapping the brittle links, does thorough reele
And to the rest the open'd passage shew.
Monke from the bank the dismall Sight does view.
Our feather'd Gallants, which came down that day
To be spectators safe of the new Play,
Leave him alone when first they hear the Gun
(*Cornb'ry* the fleetest) and to *London* run.
Our Seamen, whom no Danger's shape could fright,
Unpaid refuse to mount our Ships for spight,
Or to their fellows swim on board the *Dutch*,
Which show the tempting metall in their clutch.
Oft had he sent of *Duncome* and of *Legg*
Canon and Powder, but in vain, to beg:
And *Upnor-Castle's* ill-defended Wall,
Now needfull, does for ammunition call.
He finds, wheres'ere he Succor might expect,
Confusion, Folly, Treach'ry, Feare, Neglect.
But when the *Royal Charles* (what rage, what grief!)
He saw seis'd, and could give her no releif –
That sacred Keele, which had, as he, restor'd
His exil'd *Soveraign* on its happy board,
And thence the *Brittish Admirall* became,
Crown'd for that merit with their *Master's* Name,
That Pleasure-boat of War, in whose dear Side

Secure so oft he had his Foe defy'd,
Now a cheap spoyle and the mean Victor's slave,
Taught the *Dutch* Colors from its Top to wave –
Of former gloryes the reproachfull thought,
With present shame compar'd, his Mind distraught.
Such, from *Euphrates* bank, a Tygresse fell
After the robber for her Whelps doth Yell;
But sees inrag'd the River flow between;
Frustrate Revenge, and Love, by losse more keen,
At her own Breast her uselesse claws does arme:
She tears her self since him she can not harme.

   The Guards, plac'd for the Chain's and Fleet's defence,
Long since were fled on many a feign'd pretense.
Daniel had there adventur'd, Man of might;
Sweet *Painter*, draw his Picture while I write.
Paint him of Person tall, and big of bone,
Large limms, like Ox not to be kill'd but shown.
Scarse can burnt Iv'ry feigne an hair so black,
Or face so red, thine Oker and thy Lack.
Mix a vain terror in his martiall looke,
And all those lines by which men are mistooke;
But when, by Shame constrain'd to goe on board,
He heard how the wild Canon nearer roar'd,
And saw himself confin'd like sheep in pen,
Daniel then thought he was in Lion's den;
And when the frightfull fire-ships he saw,
Pregnant with Sulphur, to him nearer draw;

Captain, Lieutenant, Ensigne, all make haste
Ere in the Firy Furnace they be cast:
Three Children tall, unsing'd, away they row
Like *Shadrack*, *Mesheck*, and *Abednego*.

Not so brave *Douglas*, on whose lovely chin
The early Down but newly did begin,
And modest Beauty yet his Sex did veile,
While envious Virgins hope he is a Male.
His yellow Locks curle back themselves to seek,
Nor other Courtship knew but to his Cheek.
Oft as he in chill *Eske* or *Seine* by night
Harden'd and cool'd his limms, so soft, so white,
Among the reeds, to be espy'd by him
The Nymphs would rustle, he would forward swim.
They sigh'd and said, "Fond Boy, why so untame,
That fly'st Loves fires, reserv'd for other Flame?"
Fix'd on his Ship, he fac'd that horrid Day,
And wonder'd much at those that run away;
Nor other Fear himself could comprehend
Than lest *Heav'n* fall ere thither he ascend,
But intertains the while his Time too short
With birding at the *Dutch* as if in sport,
Or waves his Sword, and could he then conjure
Within its circle, knows himself secure.
The fatall Bark him boards with grappling fire,
And safely through its Port the *Dutch* retire:
That precious Life he yet disdains to save,

Or with known Art to try the gentle wave.
Much him the Honors of his ancient Race
Inspire, nor would he his own Deeds deface,
And secret Joy in his calm Soule does rise
That *Monk* looks on to see how *Douglas* dyes.
Like a glad Lover the fierce Flames he meets,
And tryes his first embraces in their Sheets.
His shape exact, which the bright Flames infold,
Like the Sun's Statue stands of burnisht Gold.
Round the transparent Fire about him glows,
As the clear Ambar on the Bee does close;
And as on Angell's heads their Gloryes shine,
His burning Locks adorn his Face divine.
But when in his immortall Mind he felt
His alt'ring Form and soder'd limms to melt,
Down on the Deck he lay'd himself and dy'd,
With his dear Sword reposing by his Side
And, on the flaming plank, so rests his Head
As one that's warm'd himself and gon to bed.
His Ship burns down and with his Reliques sinks,
And the sad stream beneath his Ashes drinks.
Fortunate Boy! If either Pencills fame,
Or if my Verse can propagate thy Name,
When *Œta* and *Alcides* are forgot,
Our *English* youth shall sing the valiant *Scott*.

    Each Dolefull Day still with fresh losse returns:
The *Loyall London* now a third time burns,

And the true *Royall Oake* and *Royall James*,
Ally'd in Fate, increase with theirs her Flames.
Of all our Navy none should now survive,
But that the Ships themselves were taught to dive,
And the Kind River in its creek them hides,
Fraughting their pierced Keels with oozy tides.

　　Up to the *Bridge* contagious Terror strook:
The *Tow'r* it self with the near Danger shook,
And were not *Ruyter's* maw with ravage cloy'd,
Ev'n *London's* ashes had been then destroy'd.
Officious Fear, however, to prevent
Our losse does so much more our losse augment:
The *Dutch* had robb'd those jewells of the *Crowne*;
Our Merchant-men, lest they be burnt, we drown.
So when the Fire did not enough devoure,
The Houses were demolish't near the *Tow'r*.
Those Ships that yearly from their teeming Howle
Unloaded here the Birth of either Pole –
Furrs from the North, and silver from the West,
Wines from the South, and spices from the East,
From *Gambo* Gold, and from the *Ganges* Gemms –
Take a short voyadge underneath the *Thames*,
Once a deep River, now with Timber floor'd,
And shrunk, least navigable, to a Ford.

　　Now (nothing more at *Chatham* left to burn)
The *Holland* squadron leisurely return,
And, spight of *Ruperts* and of *Albermarles*,

To *Ruyter's* Triumph lead the captive *Charles*.
The pleasing Sight he often does prolong:
Her Masts erect, tough Chordage, Timbers strong,
Her moving Shapes, all these he does survey,
And all admires, but most his easy Prey.
The Seamen search her all within, without:
Viewing her strength, they yet their conquest doubt;
Then with rude shouts, secure, the Aire they vex,
With gamesome Joy insulting on her Decks.
Such the fear'd *Hebrew*, captive, blinded, shorn,
Was led about in sport, the publick scorn.

    Black Day accurst! on thee let no man hale
Out of the Port, or dare to hoise a saile,
Nor row a boat in thy unlucky houre.
Thee, the years monster, let thy Dam devoure:
And constant Time, to keep his course yet right,
Fill up thy space with a redoubled Night.
When aged *Thames* was bound with fetters base,
And Medway chast ravisht before his Face,
And their dear offspring murder'd in their Sight,
Thou and thy fellows held'st the odious Light.
Sad change since first that happy pair was wed,
When all the Rivers grac'd their nuptiall Bed,
And *Father Neptune* promis'd to resigne
His Empire old to their immortall Line!
Now with vain grief their vainer hopes they rue,
Themselves dishonor'd, and the Gods untrue,

And to each other, helplesse couple, mone,
As the sad Tortoyse for the Sea does groan.
But most they for their darling *Charles* complain,
And, were it burnt, yet lesse would be their pain.
To see that fatall pledge of Sea-command
Now in the Ravisher *De-Ruyter's* hand,
The *Thames* roar'd, swooning *Medway* turn'd her tide,
And, were they mortall, both for grief had dy'd.

 The *Court* in farthing yet it self does please,
And female *Stuart*, there, rules the foure Seas,
But Fate does still accumulate our Woes,
And *Richmond* her commands, as *Ruyter* those.

 After this Losse, to rellish discontent,
Someone must be accus'd by Punishment.
All our miscarriages on *Pett* must fall:
His Name alone seems fit to answer all.
Whose Counsell first did this mad War beget?
Who all Commands sold through the Navy? *Pett.*
Who would not follow when the *Dutch* were bet?
Who treated out the time at *Bergen? Pett.*
Who the *Dutch Fleet* with Storms disabled met?
And, rifling Prizes, them neglected? *Pett.*
Who with false news prevented the *Gazette*,
The Fleet divided, writ for Rupert? *Pett.*
Who all our Seamen cheated of their Debt,
And all our Prizes who did swallow? *Pett.*
Who did advise no Navy out to set,

And who the Forts left unrepaired? *Pett.*
Who to supply with Powder did forget
Languard, Sheernesse, Graves-end, and *Upnor? Pett.*
Who all our Ships expos'd in *Chatham's* Net?
Who should it be but the *Fanatick Pett.*
Pett, the Sea Architect, in making Ships,
Was the first cause of all these Navall slips:
Had he not built, none of these Faults had bin;
If no Creation, there had been no Sin.
But, his great Crime, one Boat away he sent:
That lost our Fleet, and did our Flight prevent.

    Then, that Reward might in its turn take place,
And march with Punishment in equall pace:
Southampton dead, much of the *Treasure's* Care,
And place in Counsell fell to *Duncome's* share.
All men admir'd he to that pitch could fly:
Powder ne'r blew man up so soon so high,
But sure his late good husbandry in Petre
Show'd him to manage the *Exchequer* meeter;
And who the Forts would not vouchsafe a corn,
To lavish the *King's* Money more would scorn.
Who hath no Chimneys, to give all is best;
And ablest Speaker, who of Law has least;
Who lesse Estate, for Treasurer most fit,
And for a Couns'lor, he that has least Wit.
But the true Cause was, that, in's Brother *May,*
Th' *Exchequer* might the Privy-purse obey.

But now draws near the *Parliament's* return:
Hide and the *Court* again begin to mourn;
Frequent in Counsell, earnest in Debate,
All Arts they try how to prolong its Date.
Grave Primate *Shelden* (much in preaching there)
Blames the last Session and this more does fear:
With *Boynton* or with *Middleton* 'twere sweet,
But with a *Parliament* abhors to meet
And thinks 'twill ne'r be well within this Nation
Till it be govern'd by a *Convocation*.
But in the *Thames's* mouth still *Ruyter* laid;
The Peace not sure, new Army must be paid.
Hide saith he hourly waits for a dispatch;
Harry came post just as he shew'd his Watch,
All to agree the Articles were clear,
The *Holland* Fleet and *Parliament* so near;
Yet, *Harry* must jobb back, and all mature,
Binding, ere th' *Houses* meet, the *Treaty* sure.
And 'twixt Necessity and Spight, till then,
Let them come up so to goe down agen.

   Up ambles Country Justice on his Pad,
And Vest bespeaks to be more seemly clad.
Plain Gentlemen in Stage-Coach are ore thrown,
And Deputy-Lieutenants in their own.
The portly Burgesse, through the Weather hot,
Does for his Corporation sweat and trott;
And all with Sun and Choler come adust

And threaten *Hide* to raise a greater Dust.
But, fresh as from the Mint, the Courtiers fine
Salute them, smiling at their vain designe,
And *Turner* gay up to his Pearch does march
With Face new bleach't, smoothen'd and stiffe
    with starche;
Tells them he at *Whitehall* had took a turn,
And for three Dayes thence moves them to adjourn.
"Not so!" quoth *Tomkins*, and straight drew his Tongue.
Trusty as steele, that always ready hung;
And so, proceeding in his motion warm,
Th' Army soon rais'd he doth as soon disarme.
True Trojan! While this Town can girles afford,
And long as Cider lasts in *Hereford*,
The Girles shall always kisse thee though grown old,
And in eternall Healths thy Name be troll'd.
    Meanwhile the certain News of Peace arrives
At *Court*, and so reprieves their guilty Lives.
Hide orders *Turner* that he should come late,
Lest some new *Tomkins* spring a fresh Debate.
The *King* that day rais'd early from his rest,
Expects, as at a Play, till *Turner's* drest.
At last, together *Eaton* come and he:
No Diall more could with the Sun agree.
The *Speaker*, summon'd, to the *Lords* repairs,
Nor gave the *Commons* leave to say their pray'rs,
But like his Pris'ners to the Bar them led,

Where mute they stand to hear their sentence read:
Trembling with Joy and Fear, *Hide* them prorogues,
And had almost mistook and call'd them Rogues.
  Dear *Painter*, draw this *Speaker* to the foot:
Where Pencill can not, there my Pen shall do't;
That may his Body, this his Mind explain.
Paint him in Golden Gown, with Mace's Brain,
Bright Hair, fair Face, obscure and dull of Head,
Like Knife with Iv'ry haft and edge of Lead.
At Pray'rs, his Eyes turn up the pious white,
But all the while His Private-Bill's in sight.
In Chair, he smoking sits like Master-Cook,
And a Poll-Bill does like his Apron look.
Well was he skill'd to season any question,
And made a sawce fit for *Whitehall's* digestion;
Whence ev'ry day, the Palat more to tickle,
Court-mushrumps ready are, sent in in pickle.
When Grievance urg'd, he swells like squatted Toad,
Frisks, like a Frog, to croak a Taxes load;
His patient Pisse he could hold longer then
An Urinall, and sit like any Hen;
At Table jolly as a Country-Host
And soaks his Sack with *Norfolk* like a Toast:
At Night than *Chanticleer* more brisk and hot,
And *Sergeant's* Wife serves him for *Pertelott.*
  Paint last the *King* and a dead shade of Night
Only dispers'd by a weak Taper's light,

And those bright gleams that dart along and glare
From his clear Eyes (yet these too dark with Care).
There, as in the calm horror all alone
He wakes and muses of th' uneasy Throne,
Raise up a sudden shape with Virgin's Face:
(Though ill agree her posture, hour, or place)
Naked as born, and her round Arms behind
With her own Tresses interwove and twin'd;
Her Mouth lockt up, a blind before her Eyes;
Yet from beneath the Veile her blushes rise,
And silent Tears her secret anguish speak;
Her Heart throbbs and with very shame would break.
The Object strange in him no terror mov'd;
He wonder'd first, then pity'd, then he loved,
And with kind hand does the coy Vision presse,
Whose Beauty greater seem'd by her distresse,
But soon shrunk back, chill'd with her touch so cold,
And th' airy Picture vanish't from his hold.
In his deep thoughts the wonder did increase;
And he divin'd, 'twas *England* or the *Peace*.

Expresse him startling next with listning eare,
As one that some unusuall noyse does hear:
With Canon, Trumpets, Drums, his door surround,
But let some other Painter draw the sound.
Thrice did he rise, thrice the vain Tumult fled,
But again thunders when he lyes in Bed.
His mind secure does the known stroke repeat

And finds the Drums *Lewis's* March did beat.
    Shake then the room and all his curtains tear
And with blew streaks infect the Taper clear,
While the pale Ghosts his Eye does fixt admire
Of Grandsire *Harry* and of *Charles* his Sire.
Harry sits down, and in his open Side
The grisly Wound reveals of which he dy'd;
And ghastly *Charles*, turning his collar low,
The purple thread about his Neck does show,
Then, whisp'ring to his Son in words unheard,
Through the lockt door both of them disappear'd.
The wondrous Night the pensive *King* revolves,
And rising straight on *Hide's* Disgrace resolves.
    At his first step, he *Castlemain* does find,
Bennet and *Coventry*, as 'twere design'd.
And they, not knowing, the same thing propose
Which his hid Mind did in its depths inclose.
Through their feign'd speech their secret Hearts
        he knew:
To her own Husband, *Castlemain* untrue;
False to his Master *Bristoll, Arlington*;
And *Coventry*, falser than any one,
Who to the Brother, Brother would betray,
Nor therefore trusts himself to such as they.
His Father's Ghost too whisper'd him one note,
That who does cut his purse will cut his throat,
But in wise anger he their crimes forbears,

As Thiev's repriev'd for Executioners;
While *Hide*, provok't, his foaming tusk does whet
To prove them Traytors, and himself the *Pett*.
   Painter, adieu, how well our Arts agree!
Poetique Picture, painted Poetry!
But this great Worke is for our *Monarch* fit,
And henceforth *Charles* only to *Charles* shall sit.
His master-hand the Ancients shall outdo
Himself the *Painter* and the *Poet* too.

To the King

   So his bold Tube Man to the Sun apply'd
And spots unknown to the bright Star descry'd:
Show'd they obscure him while too near they please,
And seem his Courtiers, are but his disease.
Through optick Trunk the Planet seem'd to hear
And hurles them off e'er since in his Careere.
   And you, *Great Sir*, that with him Empire share,
Sun of our World, as he the *Charles* is There:
Blame not the Muse that brought those spots to sight
Which, in your Splendor hid, corrode your Light.
(Kings in the Country oft have gone astray,
Nor of a Peasant scorn'd to learn the Way).
   Would She the unattended Throne reduce,
Banishing Love, Trust, Ornament, and Use,
Better it were to live in Cloyster's lock,
Or in faire Fields to rule the easy Flock.

She blames them only who the *Court* restraine,
And, where all *England* serves, themselves would reigne.

  Bold and accurst are they that all this while
Have strove to isle our *Monarch* from his *Isle*,
And to improve themselves, on false pretense,
About the *Common-Prince* have rais'd a Fense;
The *Kingdom* from the *Crown* distinct would see
And peele the Barke to burn at last the Tree.
(But *Ceres* Corn, and *Flora* is the Spring,
Bachus is Wine, the *Country* is the *King*).

  Not so does Rust insinuating weare,
Nor Powder so the vaulted Bastion teare,
Nor Earthquake so an hollow Isle o'erwhelm,
As scratching Courtiers undermine a Realme
And through the Palace's Foundations bore,
Burr'wing themselves to hoord their guilty store.
The smallest Vermine make the greatest Waste,
And a poor Warren once a City ras'd.

  But they whom, born to Virtue and to Wealth,
Nor Guilt to Flatt'ry binds, nor Want to Stealth;
Whose gen'rous Conscience and whose Courage high
Does with clear Counsells their Large Soules supply;
That serve the *King* with their Estates and Care,
And as in Love on *Parliments* can stare,
(Where few the Number, Choice is there lesse hard):
Give us this *Court* and rule without a Guard.

CLARINDON'S HOUSE-WARMING

When *Clarindon* had discern'd before hand
(As the Cause can eas'ly foretell the Effect)
At once three deluges threatning our land,
'Twas the season, he thought, to turn Architect.

Us *Mars* and *Apollo* and *Vulcan* consume,
While he, the betrayer of *England* and *Flander*,
Like the Kings-fisher chuses to build in the brume,
And nestles in flames like the Salamander.

But (observing that Mortalls run often behind,
So unreasonable are the rates that they buy at)
His omnipotence, therefore, much rather design'd
How he might create an House with a fiat.

He had read of *Rhodopis*, a Lady of *Thrace*,
That was digg'd up so often ere she did marry:
And wisht that his Daughter had had as much Grace
To erect him a Pyramid out of her Quarry:

But then (recollecting how harper *Amphion*
Made *Thebes* danse aloft while he fidled and sung)
He thought (as an instrument he was most free on)
To build with the Jews-trump of his own toungue.

Yet a Precedent fitter in *Virgil* he found
Of *African Poltney* and *Tyrian Dide*
That she begg'd, for a Palace, so much of his ground
As might carry the measure and name of an Hide.

Thus daily his gowty invention he paind;
And all for to save the expense of brick-bat,
That Engine so fatall which *Denham* had brain'd
And too much resembled his Wife's Chocolatt.

But while these devices he all does compare
None solid enough seem'd for this Thong-caster:
He himself would not dwell in a Castle of aire,
Though he'd built full many an one for his *Master*.

Already he'd got all our money and cattell
To buy us for slaves and to purchase our lands:
What *Joseph* by famine, he wrought by Sea-battell;
Nay scarce the Priests portion could scape from
        his hands.

And, hence-forth, like *Pharao*, that Israel prest
To make mortar and brick yet allow'd 'm no straw,
He car'd not though *Egypt's* ten Plagues us infest,
So he could but to build make that Policy Law.

The *Scotch-forts* and *Dunkirke*, but that they were sold,
He would have demolisht to raise up his Walls;
Nay even from *Tangier* sent back for the Mold,
But that he had nearer the Stone of *St. Pauls*.

His wood would come in at the easiest rate,
As long as the yards had a deale or a sparre:
His freind in the Navy would not be ingrate
To grudge him for timber, who fram'd him the War.

To proceed on this Moddell, he call'd in his *Allans* –
The two *Allans* when joviall that ply him with galons,
The two *Allans* that serve his blind justice for balance,
The two *Allans* that serve his injustice for talons.

They approv'd it thus far and said it was fine,
Yet his *Lordship* to finish it would be unable
Unlesse all abroad he divulg'd the designe:
But his House then would grow like a vegetable.

His rent would no more in arreare run to *Worster*;
He should dwell more nobly and cheaper too at home,
While into a fabrick the presents would muster,
As by hooke and by crooke the world clustered
      of Atome.

He lik'd the advice and they soon it assay'd;
And presents crowd headlong to give good example;
So the Bribes overlayd her that *Rome* once betrayd;
The Tribes ne'r contributed so to the Temple.

Streight Judges, Priests, Bishops (true sons of the *Seale*)
Sinners, Governors, Farmers, Banquiers, Patentees
Bring in the whole milk of a yeare at a meale:
As all *Chedder* Dairies club to th' incorporate Cheese.

Bulteale's, Bealin's, Morley's, Wren's fingers with telling
Were shrivled, and *Clutterbook's, Eager's,* and *Kipps*:
Since the *Act of Oblivion* was never such selling
As at this benevolence out of the snipps.

'Twas then that the Chimney contractors he smok'd
Nor would take his belov'd Canary in kind:
But he swore that the Patent should ne'r be revok'd,
Nor, would the whole *Parliament* kisse him behind.

Like *Jove* under *Ætna* orewhelming the *Giant*,
For foundation he *Bristoll* sunk in the earth's bowell;
And *St. John* must now for the Leads be compliant,
Or his right hand shall else be hackt off with a trowell.

For surveying the building *Prat* did the feate;
But for the expense he rely'd upon *Wost'holme*,

Who sat heretofore at the *Kings* receit,
But receiv'd now and paid the *Chancellor's* Custome.

By subsidyes thus both clerick and laick,
And of matter profane cemented with holy,
He finisht at last his Palace mosaick;
By a modell more excellent than *Leslye's-folly*.

And upon the Tarras to consummate all,
A Lantern, like *Fauxe's*, surveys the burnt town;
And shows, on the top, by the regall gold ball,
Where you are to expect the Scepter and Crowne.

Fond City its rubbish and ruines that builds,
Like vain Chymists, a flowr from its ashes returning;
Your Metropolis-house is in St. James's feilds
And till there you remove you shall never leave burning.

This Temple of Warre and of Peace is the shrine
Where our *Idoll of State* sits ador'd and accurst:
And to hansell his Altar and nostrills divine
Greate *Buckingham's* Sacrifice must be the first.

Now some, as all Builders must censure abide,
Throw dust on its front and blame situation:
And others as much reprehend his backside,
As too narrow by farre for his expatiation.

But do not consider, in processe of times,
That, for name's sake, he may with *Hide-park* it enlarge;
And with what convenience he hence for his crimes
At *Tyburn* may land, and spare the *Tow'r-barge*.

Or rather, how wisely his Stall was built near,
Lest with driving too farre, his tallow impaire;
When like the whole Ox, for publick good cheare
He comes to be roasted next St. James's Faire.

THE VOWS

When the plate was at pawn and the fob at an eb
And the Spider might weave in our stomack its web,
    Our Stomach as empty as braine,
      Then *Charles* without Acre
      Made these vows to his *Maker*
    If ere he saw *England* againe.

I will have a Religion then all of mine own
Where *Papist* from *Protestant* shall not be known,
But if it grow troublesome I will have none.

I will have a fine *Parliament* alwayes to freind
That shall furnish me Treasure as fast as I spend,
But when they will not they shall be at an end.

I will have as fine Bishops as were e'er made with hands
With consciences flexible to my commands,
But if they displease me I will have all their lands.

I will have my fine *Chancellor* bear all the sway
Yet if men should clamour I'll pack him away
And yet call him home again soon as I may.

I will have a fine Navy to conquer the seas
And the *Dutch* shall give caution for their Provinces,
But if they should beat me I will do what they please.

I will have a new *London* instead of the old,
With wide streets and uniforme of mine own mold,
But if they build it too fast, I will soon make them hold.

I will have a fine Son (in making though marr'd)
If not or'e a Kingdome to reigne or'e my guard
And Successor, if not to me, to *Gerrard*.

I will have a fine *Court*, with ne're an old face
And always who beards me shall have the next grace,
And I either will vacate or buy him a place.

I will have a *Privy Councill* to sit always still,
I will have a fine *Junto* to do what I will,
I will have two fine *Secretaryes* pisse through one quill.

I will have a *Privy-purse* without a controll,
I will wink all the while my Revenue is stole,
And if any be question'd I'll answer the whole.

But whatever it cost I will have a fine whore
As bold as *Alce Pierce* and as faire as *Jane Shore*,
And when I am weary of her I'll have more.

Of my Pimp, I will make my *Ministre premier*,
My bawd shall Ambassadors send far and near,
And my Wench shall dispose of the *Congé d'eslire*.

If this please not I'll reigne upon any condition,
Miss and I will both learn to live on exhibition,
And I'll first put the *Church* then my *Crown* in
      Commission.

I will have a fine Tunick, a shash and a Vest
Though not rule like the *Turk* yet I will be so drest
And who knows but the mode may soon bring in
      the rest?

I will have a fine pond and a pretty Decoy
Where the Ducks and the Drakes may their
      freedoms enjoy
And quack in their language still, *Vive le Roy*.